Have YE Not Read

Authored by:
Pastor Scott Hanks, Ph D
Heritage Baptist Church

Mercy & TRUTH
M•I•N•I•S•T•R•I•E•S
1781 E. 800 Road
Lawrence, KS 66049
(A ministry of Heritage Baptist Church)

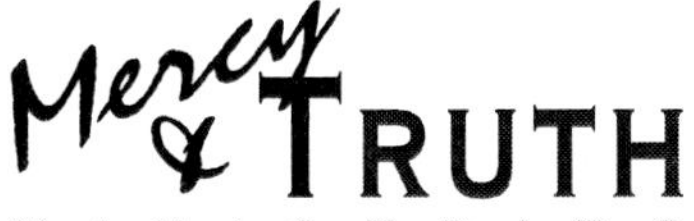

Scripture and answers taken from the
King James Bible.

Credits
Layout and Editing: Joy Smith
Cover Design: Carrie Selim

How to use this Bible study

What do these passages mean?
Briefly write an overview of the passage content.

How does it apply to me?
Write down how you can apply a verse or principle to your Christian life.

Questions from the text.
Answer the question as you finish reading each chapter.

Messages preached from text.
Use this space to write outlines or special decisions that you make during preaching services. These will help you later when you read that portion of scripture in your devotions.

And have ye not read this
Scripture; The stone which
the builders rejected is become
the head of the corner:
Mark 12:10

Preface

Paul admonished Timothy "...give attendance to reading,..." I Timothy 4:13. Reading the Word of God on a daily basis is of utmost importance. Reading the Bible provides us with the spiritual food that we need to combat the enemies of the Christian - the world, the flesh, and the devil.

Each year Mercy & Truth features a new devotional book with new questions for each chapter in the Bible. Writing down the lessons you learn from your reading can be a help to you and a blessing to others as you share how the Lord has spoken to you.

Have Ye Not Read is a tool to help you stay on track in your Bible reading, and help you get the most out of it. It is my prayer that you will take the opportunity each day to let the Lord speak to you through His Word.

- Scott Hanks

Questions from text:

Chapter 1: The lights in the heavens that divide the day and night would be for what four things? ____________________
Chapter 2: Who named every living creature? ____________________
Chapter 3: God told Adam, "for dust thou art, and unto ____________________ shalt thou return."

What does this passage mean?

How does this apply to me?

Messages preached from text:

Questions from text:

Chapter 4: Who was an instructer of every artificer in brass and iron? ______
______
Chapter 5: What did Enoch do "after" he begat Methuselah? ______
______
Chapter 6: Of what type of wood was the ark to be made? ______
Chapter 7: Who shut Noah in the ark? ______

What does this passage mean?

How does this apply to me?

Messages preached from text:

Questions from text:

Chapter 8: What four things did God say "shall not cease?" ______________

____

Chapter 9: Of whom was Ham the father? ______________

Chapter 10: In whose day was the earth divided? ______________

Chapter 11: What did the people at the tower of Babel use for stone and morter? ______________

What does this passage mean?

How does this apply to me?

Messages preached from text:

Questions from text:

Chapter 12: Why did God plague Pharaoh's house? ____________________

____

Chapter 13: When Abram and Lot separated from each other, where did Abram dwell? ____________________

Chapter 14: How many trained servants did Abram have? ____________________

Chapter 15: What two rivers would be the borders of the land God promised Abram? ____________________

What does this passage mean?

How does this apply to me?

Messages preached from text:

Questions from text:

Chapter 16: What name did Hagar call the Lord that spake unto her? ____

Chapter 17: Who would beget twelve princes? ____

Chapter 18: What did the Lord say about Sodom and Gomorrah's sin? ____

What does this passage mean?

How does this apply to me?

Messages preached from text:

Questions from text:

Chapter 19: Why did Lot's wife become a pillar of salt? ________________

____

*Chapter 20: How many pieces of silver did Abimelech give Abraham?*________

Chapter 21: What did the lad Ishmael become? ________________

What does this passage mean?

How does this apply to me?

Messages preached from text:

Questions from text:

Chapter 22: What did Abraham call the place where he offered a ram, instead of Isaac? ______________________

Chapter 23: The children of Heth said that Abraham was a mighty ________ ________.

Chapter 24: Rebekah gave water to how many camels? ________________

What does this passage mean?

How does this apply to me?

Messages preached from text:

Questions from text:

Chapter 25: What happened to Isaac after Abraham died? ______________

____

Chapter 26: How old was Esau when he married? ______________

What does this passage mean?

How does this apply to me?

Messages preached from text:

Questions from text:

Chapter 27: Rebekah told Jacob to flee ________________________ from his brother Esau?

Chapter 28: What did Jacob call the place where he dreamed? __________

Chapter 29: What two descriptions are given of Rachel? ________________

What does this passage mean?

How does this apply to me?

Messages preached from text:

Questions from text:

Chapter 30: To whom did God hearken when He opened Rachel's womb?

____

Chapter 31: How many years was Jacob with Laban? ______________

What does this passage mean?

How does this apply to me?

Messages preached from text:

Questions from text:

Chapter 32: To what was Jacob's name changed? ______________________

Chapter 33: What was the name of the altar Jacob erected? ____________

Chapter 34: Who asked Jacob to allow his son to marry Jacob's daughter?

____

What does this passage mean?

How does this apply to me?

Messages preached from text:

Questions from text:

Chapter 35: What was the name of the son born to Rachel? ______________

Chapter 36: For what was Anah known? ______________________________

____

What does this passage mean?

How does this apply to me?

Messages preached from text:

Questions from text:

Chapter 37: Why did Israel love Joseph more than all his children? ________

____

Chapter 38: Which child of Tamar had a scarlet thread around his hand?

____

Chapter 39: What did the keeper of the prison commit to Joseph? ________

____

What does this passage mean?

How does this apply to me?

Messages preached from text:

Questions from text:

Chapter 40: Who did Joseph serve? ______________________
Chapter 41: Why did Joseph name his second child Ephraim? __________
____
Chapter 42: Joseph accused his brothers three times of being what? ______

What does this passage mean?

How does this apply to me?

Messages preached from text:

Questions from text:

Chapter 43: When Joseph's brothers returned to Egypt, they took double of what? ______________________

Chapter 44: Judah said Joseph was "even as" whom? ______________

What does this passage mean?

How does this apply to me?

Messages preached from text:

Questions from text:

Chapter 45: Joseph said, "It was not _____ that sent me hither, but _____."
Chapter 46: What did Pharaoh send to transport Jacob to Egypt? ________
Chapter 47: What did people use to buy food, when money and cattle failed?
____

What does this passage mean?

How does this apply to me?

Messages preached from text:

Questions from text:

Chapter 48: Where did Jacob say God blessed him? ____________________

Chapter 49: "The sceptre shall not depart from____________________."

Chapter 50: Who stayed in Goshen when Joseph went to bury his father?

____

What does this passage mean?

How does this apply to me?

Messages preached from text:

Questions from text:

Chapter 1: What did Pharaoh charge his people to do with every Israelite son that was born? __________

Chapter 2: What was the name of Moses' son? __________

Chapter 3: What was God sure the king of Egypt would not do? __________

What does this passage mean?

How does this apply to me?

Messages preached from text:

Questions from text:

Chapter 4: What was the first sign Moses was to use to prove that God sent him? ____________________

Chapter 5: Who said, "Who is the Lord?" ____________________

Chapter 6: What was the name of Moses' father? ____________________

What does this passage mean?

How does this apply to me?

Messages preached from text:

Questions from text:

Chapter 7: Pharaoh would not hearken because his heart was __________.
Chapter 8: What did God turn into lice? ____________________
Chapter 9: For what reason did God raise up Pharaoh? ________________

What does this passage mean?

How does this apply to me?

Messages preached from text:

Questions from text:

Chapter 10: What did the locusts eat? ______________________

____

Chapter 11: What were the Israelites to borrow from their neighbours?

____

Chapter 12: How many years did the children of Israel sojourn in Egypt?

____

What does this passage mean?

How does this apply to me?

Messages preached from text:

Questions from text:

Chapter 13: When the Lord led Israel out of Egypt, why didn't He lead them through the land of the Philistines? ______________________________

Chapter 14: What was a wall unto the children of Israel on their right and left? ______________________________

What does this passage mean?

How does this apply to me?

Messages preached from text:

Questions from text:

Chapter 15: "The Lord is my ________________ and ________________."
Chapter 16: How many years did the children of Israel eat manna? ________
Chapter 17: How long did the Lord say He would have war with Amalek?
____

What does this passage mean?

How does this apply to me?

Messages preached from text:

Questions from text:

Chapter 18: What was the name of Moses' father-in-law? ______________
Chapter 19: God told the Israelites that if they obeyed His voice they would be a peculiar ____________________.
Chapter 20: Why did God tell Israel to not go up by steps to His altar?
____

What does this passage mean?

How does this apply to me?

Messages preached from text:

Questions from text:

Chapter 21: What happened to an ox that killed a person? ______________

____

Chapter 22: Who were the children of Israel not to suffer to live? ______

Chapter 23: Who did God say He would not justify? ______________

What does this passage mean?

How does this apply to me?

Messages preached from text:

Questions from text:

Chapter 24: When Moses went up into the mount, what covered the mount?

____

Chapter 25: God told Moses, "Let them make me a ______________; that I may dwell among them."

Chapter 26: How many curtains were to be "a covering upon the tabernacle"?

____

What does this passage mean?

How does this apply to me?

Messages preached from text:

Questions from text:

Chapter 27: What was to be blue, and purple, and scarlet, and fine twined linen? ____________________

Chapter 28: The holy garments for Aaron were made for ________________ and for ________________.

What does this passage mean?

How does this apply to me?

Messages preached from text:

Questions from text:

Chapter 29: How many days did it take to consecrate Aaron and his sons?

____

Chapter 30: What was between the tabernacle of the congregation and the altar? _______________

What does this passage mean?

How does this apply to me?

Messages preached from text:

Questions from text:

Chapter 31: For what was an Israelite to be put to death? ____________

____

Chapter 32: From whom was the Lord willing to make a great nation?

____

Chapter 33: The Lord spoke to Moses as a man speaketh to his ____________.

What does this passage mean?

How does this apply to me?

Messages preached from text:

Questions from text:

Chapter 34: What will God "by no means" do? ________________________
Chapter 35: "They came, both men and women, as many as were ________
____________________ *hearted."*

What does this passage mean?

How does this apply to me?

Messages preached from text:

Questions from text:

Chapter 36: The stuff the people made for the work was too ____________.
Chapter 37: What was the length and breadth of the incense altar? ________

Chapter 38: All the hangings of the court were made of what? ___________

What does this passage mean?

How does this apply to me?

Messages preached from text:

Questions from text:

Chapter 39: What was between the bells on the hem of the priests' garment?

____

Chapter 40: When was the tabernacle reared up? ______________________________

____

What does this passage mean?

How does this apply to me?

Messages preached from text:

Questions from text:

Chapter 1: Where were the priests supposed to sprinkle the blood from the burnt offering? ______________________________

Chapter 2: What was not to be lacking from the meat offering? __________

Chapter 3: What two types of animals could be offered for a peace offering?

____

Chapter 4: If the whole ____________________ *sinned through ignorance they were to bring a sin offering.*

What does this passage mean?

How does this apply to me?

Messages preached from text:

Questions from text:

Chapter 5: "He shall bring his ____________________ offering unto the Lord for his sin which he hath sinned."
Chapter 6: Where was the fire to never go out? ______________________

What does this passage mean?

How does this apply to me?

Messages preached from text:

Questions from text:

Chapter 7: Where were the priests to burn the fat? ____________________
Chapter 8: Moses sanctified the _______________ *and all that was therein.*

What does this passage mean?

How does this apply to me?

Messages preached from text:

Questions from text:

Chapter 9: What did Aaron sacrifice for himself? ________________________
Chapter 10: Who carried Nadab and Abihu out from before the sanctuary out of the camp? ________________________
Chapter 11: "I am the Lord your God: ye shall therefore ________________ yourselves."

What does this passage mean?

How does this apply to me?

Messages preached from text:

Questions from text:

Chapter 12: This chapter "is the law for her that hath" what? ____________

____

Chapter 13: With whom was a leper to dwell? ____________

What does this passage mean?

How does this apply to me?

Messages preached from text:

Questions from text:

Chapter 14: Who was the one that plagued a house with leprosy? ________
Chapter 15: God wanted Israel to separate from their uncleanness so they wouldn't defile what? ______________________________

What does this passage mean?

How does this apply to me?

Messages preached from text:

Questions from text:

Chapter 16: The goat that the Lord's lot fell on, was to be used as a ______

____

Chapter 17: What did God have Israel place upon the altar to make an atonement? ______________________________

Chapter 18: How many times is the word "uncover" mentioned? __________

What does this passage mean?

How does this apply to me?

Messages preached from text:

Questions from text:

Chapter 19: Why were the Israelites to love a stranger as themselves?

Chapter 20: Why did God separate Israel from other people? ____________

What does this passage mean?

How does this apply to me?

Messages preached from text:

Questions from text:

Chapter 21: Of whom did God say, "I the Lord do sanctify him?" ______________

____

Chapter 22: "They shall not profane the ______________ *things of the children of Israel."*

Chapter 23: What were the Israelites to bring to the priests of their harvest?

____

What does this passage mean?

How does this apply to me?

Messages preached from text:

Questions from text:

Chapter 24: How was the man killed who blasphemed the name of the Lord?

____

Chapter 25: What year was a sabbath of rest? ______________________

What does this passage mean?

How does this apply to me?

Messages preached from text:

Questions from text:

Chapter 26: If Israel would not hearken, God would punish them seven times more and "bring a ________________ upon" them.
Chapter 27: What was one of the four things that could be sanctified unto the Lord? ____

What does this passage mean?

How does this apply to me?

Messages preached from text:

Questions from text:

Chapter 1: What was one of the three qualifications in the numbering of Israel?

____

Chapter 2: On the north side shall be the standard of the camp of ________.

What does this passage mean?

How does this apply to me?

Messages preached from text:

Questions from text:

Chapter 3: How many firstborn were among the children of Israel? ________
Chapter 4: How old were those to be who worked in the tabernacle? ________

What does this passage mean?

How does this apply to me?

Messages preached from text:

Questions from text:

Chapter 5: What two things was a person supposed to do if he committed a trespass against the Lord? ______________________

Chapter 6: During a Nazarite's days of separation, what could he not eat?

____

What does this passage mean?

How does this apply to me?

Messages preached from text:

Questions from text:

Chapter 7: What was the name of the prince who offered on the seventh day? ______________________

What does this passage mean?

How does this apply to me?

Messages preached from text:

Questions from text:

Chapter 8: At what age would a Levite have to "serve no more?" ___________
Chapter 9: What would the children of Israel do when the cloud tarried long on the tabernacle? ___________
Chapter 10: The Israelites journeyed from the wilderness of Sinai, to the wilderness of ___________.

What does this passage mean?

How does this apply to me?

Messages preached from text:

Questions from text:

Chapter 11: Who was buried at Kibroth-hattaavah? ____________________
Chapter 12: Who is described as "very meek?" ________________________
Chapter 13: Ten spies brought back an ____________ *report of the land.*

What does this passage mean?

How does this apply to me?

Messages preached from text:

Questions from text:

Chapter 14: What appeared in the tabernacle when the congregation talked of stoning Caleb and Joshua? ______________________

Chapter 15: What were they supposed to put on the fringe of the borders of their garments? ______________________

What does this passage mean?

How does this apply to me?

Messages preached from text:

Questions from text:

Chapter 16: What was to be a sign unto the children of Israel? ______

______

Chapter 17: Where did God say, "I will meet with you?" ______

______

Chapter 18: What was Aaron's inheritance? ______

What does this passage mean?

How does this apply to me?

Messages preached from text:

Questions from text:

Chapter 19: What were three requirements concerning the red heifer?

____

Chapter 20: Who refused to give the children of Israel passage through their border? ____

Chapter 21: What two kings did Israel defeat in this chapter? ____________

What does this passage mean?

How does this apply to me?

Messages preached from text:

Questions from text:

Chapter 22: Why did the angel of the Lord go out to withstand Balaam?

____

Chapter 23: "God is not a man, that he should _____________."

What does this passage mean?

How does this apply to me?

Messages preached from text:

Questions from text:

Chapter 24: What did it please the Lord to do? ______________________
Chapter 25: What did Phinehas do that stayed the plague from the children of Israel? ______________________
Chapter 26: Why did Nadab and Abihu die? ______________________

____

What does this passage mean?

How does this apply to me?

Messages preached from text:

Questions from text:

Chapter 27: If a man die and have no son, to whom would his inheritance pass?

Chapter 28: During Israel's holy convocations, what manner of work was not to be done?

What does this passage mean?

How does this apply to me?

Messages preached from text:

Questions from text:

Chapter 29: "These things ye shall do unto the Lord in your set __________."
Chapter 30: The vow of a girl in her youth could be disallowed by whom?

____

Chapter 31: Who caused the children of Israel, through the counsel of Balaam, to commit trespass against the Lord? ________________________

What does this passage mean?

How does this apply to me?

Messages preached from text:

Questions from text:

Chapter 32: Why did Reuben and Gad want the land on this side of Jordan?

____

Chapter 33: When Israel passed over Jordan into the land of Canaan, what were they to "destroy?" ______________________________

What does this passage mean?

How does this apply to me?

Messages preached from text:

Questions from text:

Chapter 34: What were they supposed to take of every tribe, to divide the land by inheritance? ______________________________

Chapter 35: How many cities were to be given to the Levites? __________

Chapter 36: Every one of the children of Israel was to keep himself to what?

____

What does this passage mean?

How does this apply to me?

Messages preached from text:

Questions from text:

Chapter 1: What discouraged the heart of the people from going into the Promised Land? ________________________

Chapter 2: What two groups of people were considered great, many, and tall?

____

What does this passage mean?

How does this apply to me?

Messages preached from text:

Questions from text:

Chapter 3: Whose bedstead was nine cubits long and four cubits wide? ___

___

Chapter 4: If thou shalt seek the Lord thy God, thou shalt _______ _______.

What does this passage mean?

How does this apply to me?

Messages preached from text:

Questions from text:

Chapter 5: What did God tell Israel to "remember?" ______________________

____

Chapter 6: For what two reasons were the Israelites to do that which was right and good in the sight of the Lord? ______________________

____

Chapter 7: With whom does the Lord keep covenant and mercy? __________

____

What does this passage mean?

How does this apply to me?

Messages preached from text:

Questions from text:

Chapter 8: What did God say, "thou shalt remember?" ________________

____

Chapter 9: God did not give Israel the Promised Land because of their own ________________.

Chapter 10: What five things did God require of Israel? ________________

____

What does this passage mean?

How does this apply to me?

Messages preached from text:

Questions from text:

Chapter 11: What would Israel do if they allowed their heart to deceive them?

Chapter 12: God said it would go well with them and their children when they did what?

Chapter 13: For what reason would you stone a family relative?

What does this passage mean?

How does this apply to me?

Messages preached from text:

Questions from text:

Chapter 14: God chose Israel to be a ______________ people unto Himself.
Chapter 15: Unto which three types of people did God tell Israel, "Thou shalt open thine hand wide?" ____
Chapter 16: What month did the Lord bring Israel out of Egypt? __________

What does this passage mean?

How does this apply to me?

Messages preached from text:

Questions from text:

Chapter 17: What was an abomination to the Lord? ____________________

____

Chapter 18: The Lord thy God will raise up unto thee a ____________.

Chapter 19: What two types of people were not to be pitied? ____________

____

Chapter 20: Who would first speak to the people when they came nigh for battle? ____________________

What does this passage mean?

How does this apply to me?

Messages preached from text:

Questions from text:

Chapter 21: By whose word shall every controversy and every stroke be tried?

____

Chapter 22: When building a new house, a ____________________ *was to be built for the roof.*

Chapter 23: Israelites were not to lend to their brother with ____________.

What does this passage mean?

How does this apply to me?

Messages preached from text:

Questions from text:

Chapter 24: What did God tell the Israelites to remember about Egypt?

____

Chapter 25: God said not to muzzle the ox when he is ______________ the corn.

Chapter 26: What is the year of tithing? ______________________

Chapter 27: Cursed be he that removeth his neighbour's ______________.

What does this passage mean?

How does this apply to me?

Messages preached from text:

Questions from text:

Chapter 28: All the curses in this chapter would happen to Israel if they did not do what? ______________________

What does this passage mean?

How does this apply to me?

Messages preached from text:

Questions from text:

Chapter 29: How long did Israel's clothes and shoes not wax old? ________

Chapter 30: What did God set before Israel that day? ________

____

Chapter 31: Why would God hide His face from Israel? ________

____

What does this passage mean?

How does this apply to me?

Messages preached from text:

Questions from text:

Chapter 32: What animal that takes care of her young is as the Lord to Israel?

____

Chapter 33: What tribe of Israel would teach Israel the law? ___________

Chapter 34: How long did Israel weep for Moses after he died? ___________

What does this passage mean?

How does this apply to me?

Messages preached from text:

Questions from text:

Chapter 1: What was Joshua supposed to do day and night? ____________

____

Chapter 2: What two things did the spies tell Rahab "thou shalt" do? ______

____

Chapter 3: What did Joshua tell the people to do before the Lord would do wonders among them? ____________

What does this passage mean?

How does this apply to me?

Messages preached from text:

Questions from text:

Chapter 4: How many people from the tribes of Reuben, Gad, and the half tribe of Manasseh passed over Jordan? ______________________________

Chapter 5: What was the name of the place where God rolled away the reproach of Egypt? ______________________________

Chapter 6: Why did Rahab the harlot live? ______________________________

____

What does this passage mean?

How does this apply to me?

Messages preached from text:

Questions from text:

Chapter 7: Achan was from which tribe of Israel? ____________________
Chapter 8: How many men were to lie in ambush against the city of Ai?
____
Chapter 9: What four things did the ambassadors from Gibeon have that were old? ____________________

What does this passage mean?

How does this apply to me?

Messages preached from text:

Questions from text:

Chapter 10: Who fought for Israel? ______________________________

Chapter 11: Who was the head of all the kingdoms Joshua destroyed?

____

What does this passage mean?

How does this apply to me?

Messages preached from text:

Questions from text:

Chapter 12: What river was the border of the children of Ammon? ________

Chapter 13: Whose inheritance included half the land of the children of Ammon? ________

Chapter 14: What did Joshua give Caleb for an inheritance? ________

What does this passage mean?

How does this apply to me?

Messages preached from text:

Questions from text:

Chapter 15: Who were the three sons of Anak? ____________________

____

Chapter 16: Where were the separate cities of Ephraim located? __________

____

Chapter 17: What did the Canaanites have, that kept the children of Joseph from having more inheritance? ____________________

What does this passage mean?

How does this apply to me?

Messages preached from text:

Questions from text:

Chapter 18: What was the inheritance of the Levites? ____________

Chapter 19: What verses describe the lot and inheritance of the tribe of Zebulun? ____________

What does this passage mean?

How does this apply to me?

Messages preached from text:

Questions from text:

Chapter 20: List one of the two things that would have to happen before the slayer was able to leave the city of refuge: ______________________

Chapter 21: How many were all the cities of the Levites, within the possession of the children of Israel? ______________________

Chapter 22: Who did Joshua bless? ______________________

What does this passage mean?

How does this apply to me?

Messages preached from text:

Questions from text:

Chapter 23: What did Joshua say, "ye have done unto this day?" ______________

____

Chapter 24: What did Joshua say the Lord would do if they forsook Him and served strange gods? ______________________________

What does this passage mean?

How does this apply to me?

Messages preached from text:

Questions from text:

Chapter 1: To whom was the city of Hebron given? ______________________

Chapter 2: What did the Lord raise up that delivered Israel from their enemies?

____

Chapter 3: Whose hand prevailed against Chushan-rishathaim? ____________

____

What does this passage mean?

How does this apply to me?

Messages preached from text:

Questions from text:

Chapter 4: After the battle, how many men were left of the host of Sisera?

____

Chapter 5: What did Jael give Sisera to drink? ______________

What does this passage mean?

How does this apply to me?

Messages preached from text:

Questions from text:

Chapter 6: What "came upon Gideon?" ______________________

Chapter 7: What did the men of Ephraim bring Gideon on the other side of Jordan? ______________________

Chapter 8: With what did Gideon teach the men of Succoth? ______________________

____

What does this passage mean?

How does this apply to me?

Messages preached from text:

Questions from text:

Chapter 9: What did God send between Abimelech and the men of Shechem?

Chapter 10: Who vexed and oppressed the children of Israel?

What does this passage mean?

How does this apply to me?

Messages preached from text:

Questions from text:

Chapter 11: What came upon Jephthah before he passed over to fight the children of Ammon? ____________________

Chapter 12: Who did Jephthah say delivered the children of Ammon into his hand? ____________________

Chapter 13: What two questions did Manoah ask the angel concerning the child to be born? ____________________

What does this passage mean?

How does this apply to me?

Messages preached from text:

Questions from text:

Chapter 14: To whom did Samson say "I have not told" the riddle? ________

____

Chapter 15: When Samson was brought down from the rock to the Philistines, the cords that were upon his arms become as what? ________

____

Chapter 16: How many times does this chapter say that Samson told Delilah "all his heart?" ________

What does this passage mean?

How does this apply to me?

Messages preached from text:

Questions from text:

Chapter 17: "And the Levite was ______________ to dwell with the man."
Chapter 18: Who were priests to the tribe of Dan until the day of captivity?

____

Chapter 19: Who came to the old man's house and said, "Bring forth the man that came into thy house, that we may know him?" ______________________

____

What does this passage mean?

How does this apply to me?

Messages preached from text:

Questions from text:

Chapter 20: How many did Benjamin destroy of Israel on the first day of battle?

____

Chapter 21: What was the oath "concerning him that came not up to the Lord to Mizpeh?" ________________________________

What does this passage mean?

How does this apply to me?

Messages preached from text:

Questions from text:

Chapter 1: When Naomi returned to Bethlehem she told them to call her what?

____

Chapter 2: About how much barley did Ruth glean? ______________

Chapter 3: What did Boaz give Ruth before she returned to her mother- in-law? ______________

Chapter 4: How many elders of the city witnessed Boaz' kinsman redemption?

____

What does this passage mean?

How does this apply to me?

Messages preached from text:

Questions from text:

Chapter 1: Why did Hannah call her son Samuel? ______________________

____

Chapter 2: How many sons and daughters did Hannah have? ____________

____

Chapter 3: Who opened the doors of the house of the Lord? ____________

What does this passage mean?

How does this apply to me?

Messages preached from text:

Questions from text:

Chapter 4: What caused all Israel to shout with a great shout? ____________
____
Chapter 5: They sent the ark of God from Gath, to what city? ____________
Chapter 6: The ark came from the Philistines into whose field? ____________

What does this passage mean?

How does this apply to me?

Messages preached from text:

Questions from text:

Chapter 7: Where was Samuel's house? ______________________
Chapter 8: Samuel warned that a future king would take a tenth of what two things? ______________________
Chapter 9: True or false, Saul was from the largest tribe of Israel. ________
Chapter 10: What statement became a proverb? ______________________

____

What does this passage mean?

How does this apply to me?

Messages preached from text:

Questions from text:

Chapter 11: Where did they make Saul king? ______________________

Chapter 12: What wickedness did Samuel say they had done in the sight of the Lord? ______________________

Chapter 13: What was not found throughout all the land of Israel? ________

What does this passage mean?

How does this apply to me?

Messages preached from text:

Questions from text:

Chapter 14: What was the name of the captain of Saul's host? ____________

Chapter 15: Because Saul rejected the word of the Lord, what did God do?

____

What does this passage mean?

How does this apply to me?

Messages preached from text:

Questions from text:

Chapter 16: Who did Saul favour and love greatly? ____________________

Chapter 17: What five things that begin with the letter "s" did David take with him when fighting Goliath? ____________________

____

What does this passage mean?

How does this apply to me?

Messages preached from text:

Questions from text:

Chapter 18: Name two reasons Saul was afraid of David: ________________

____

Chapter 19: When David escaped from Saul, who did he go see? ________

____

What does this passage mean?

How does this apply to me?

Messages preached from text:

Questions from text:

Chapter 20: Why did Jonathan cause David to swear again? ______________

____

Chapter 21: Why did David flee? ______________________

Chapter 22: What three things did Ahimelech do for David? ______________

____

What does this passage mean?

How does this apply to me?

Messages preached from text:

Questions from text:

Chapter 23: Why did Saul return from pursuing David? ______________

____

Chapter 24: David compared Saul going after him to someone going after a dead ____________ *or a* ____________.

Chapter 25: Abigail said the Lord would sling out David's enemies as what?

____

What does this passage mean?

How does this apply to me?

Messages preached from text:

Questions from text:

Chapter 26: What two things did David take from Saul while he slept?

____

Chapter 27: Who thought David was his servant? ______________

Chapter 28: What happened when Saul enquired of the Lord? ______________

____

What does this passage mean?

How does this apply to me?

Messages preached from text:

Questions from text:

Chapter 29: Who said David shall not go up with us to the battle? ________

Chapter 30: To whom did David send a present? ________

Chapter 31: Who did Saul ask to kill him? ________

What does this passage mean?

How does this apply to me?

Messages preached from text:

Questions from text:

Chapter 1: How many times is the phrase "How are the mighty fallen" mentioned? ______

Chapter 2: Who would not turn aside from following after Abner? ______

Chapter 3: How many sons did David have in Hebron? ______

What does this passage mean?

How does this apply to me?

Messages preached from text:

Questions from text:

Chapter 4: What did Rechab and Baanah bring to David? ______________

____

Chapter 5: How many years did David reign as king? ______________

Chapter 6: What did David give to the whole multitude of Israel? ______________

____

What does this passage mean?

How does this apply to me?

Messages preached from text:

Questions from text:

Chapter 7: Who did God say would build a house for His name? ___________

____

Chapter 8: How many men did David kill in the valley of salt? ___________

Chapter 9: What did David restore to Mephibosheth? ___________

____

Chapter 10: To whom did David try to show kindness? ___________

What does this passage mean?

How does this apply to me?

Messages preached from text:

Questions from text:

Chapter 11: Whom did David make drunk? ______________________

Chapter 12: Of whom does it say, "the Lord loved him"? ______________

What does this passage mean?

How does this apply to me?

Messages preached from text:

Questions from text:

Chapter 13: Who told David that "Amnon only is dead"? ________________

Chapter 14: Who was praised for his beauty? ________________

What does this passage mean?

How does this apply to me?

Messages preached from text:

Questions from text:

Chapter 15: What did Absalom tell his spies to say? ____________________

Chapter 16: Ahithophel's counsel was as what? ____________________

Chapter 17: Who did Absalom make captain of the host? ____________________

What does this passage mean?

How does this apply to me?

Messages preached from text:

Questions from text:

Chapter 18: Which three men did David charge to deal gently with Absalom?

____

Chapter 19: Who "was a very great man?" ____________________

What does this passage mean?

How does this apply to me?

Messages preached from text:

Questions from text:

Chapter 20: Who killed Amasa? ______________________
Chapter 21: What did the Gibeonites want from David that they might bless the inheritance of the Lord? ______________________
Chapter 22: God's eyes are upon whom? ______________________

What does this passage mean?

How does this apply to me?

Messages preached from text:

Questions from text:

Chapter 23: Who stood in the midst of a lentil field and defended it?

____

Chapter 24: David's heart smote him after what happened? ______________

____

What does this passage mean?

How does this apply to me?

Messages preached from text:

Questions from text:

Chapter 1: Where was Solomon anointed king? ______________

Chapter 2: Who took Joab's place as captain of the host? ______________

What does this passage mean?

How does this apply to me?

Messages preached from text:

Questions from text:

Chapter 3: What two things did God give Solomon although he did not ask for them? ______

Chapter 4: What were the names of Solomon's two daughters? ______

Chapter 5: What did the Lord promise Solomon? ______

What does this passage mean?

How does this apply to me?

Messages preached from text:

Questions from text:

Chapter 6: What figures were carved on all the walls of the temple ? ______

____

Chapter 7: With what was Hiram filled? ______________________________

What does this passage mean?

How does this apply to me?

Messages preached from text:

Questions from text:

Chapter 8: What did Solomon say "hath not failed"? ____________________

____

What does this passage mean?

How does this apply to me?

Messages preached from text:

Questions from text:

Chapter 9: How many times a year did Solomon offer offerings unto the Lord?

____

Chapter 10: What people did the queen of Sheba notice were happy? ______

____

What does this passage mean?

How does this apply to me?

Messages preached from text:

Questions from text:

Chapter 11: Who is mentioned as "a mighty man of valour"? ______________

Chapter 12: Whose counsel did Rehoboam forsake? ______________

What does this passage mean?

How does this apply to me?

Messages preached from text:

Questions from text:

Chapter 13: What killed the man of God who was disobedient to the word of the Lord? ____________________

Chapter 14: When did Jeroboam's child die? ____________________

____

What does this passage mean?

How does this apply to me?

Messages preached from text:

Questions from text:

Chapter 15: What happened to Asa in his old age? ______________________

____

Chapter 16: Who killed all the house of Baasha, his kinsfolk, and his friends?

____

What does this passage mean?

How does this apply to me?

Messages preached from text:

Questions from text:

Chapter 17: How many sticks did the widow of Zarephath tell Elijah she was gathering? ______________________________

Chapter 18: How many times were the four barrels of water poured on Elijah's sacrifice? ______________________________

What does this passage mean?

How does this apply to me?

Messages preached from text:

Questions from text:

Chapter 19: Who was Elijah to anoint king over Israel? ____________________
Chapter 20: Of whom did Ahab say "he is my brother?" ____________________

What does this passage mean?

How does this apply to me?

Messages preached from text:

Questions from text:

Chapter 21: What did Ahab "sell himself to"? ______________________

Chapter 22: Where did the arrow hit the king of Israel? ______________

____

What does this passage mean?

How does this apply to me?

Messages preached from text:

Questions from text:

Chapter 1: To whom did Ahaziah send messengers to enquire whether he would recover of his disease? ______________________

Chapter 2: Out of what city did the children come who mocked Elisha?

____

Chapter 3: Who was called a "sheepmaster?" ______________________

What does this passage mean?

How does this apply to me?

Messages preached from text:

Questions from text:

Chapter 4: The Shunammite woman was described as a __________ woman.
Chapter 5: Who said "Am I God?" ____________________________________

What does this passage mean?

How does this apply to me?

Messages preached from text:

Questions from text:

Chapter 6: What did Elisha tell the king of Israel to set before the Syrian army?

____

Chapter 7: Who did the Syrians think Israel hired against them? __________

____

Chapter 8: The king asked ____________________ *about all the great things Elisha had done.*

What does this passage mean?

How does this apply to me?

Messages preached from text:

Questions from text:

Chapter 9: When Joram saw Jehu, what did he ask him? ________________
Chapter 10: To whom did Jehu say, "Come with me, and see my zeal for the Lord?" ________________

What does this passage mean?

How does this apply to me?

Messages preached from text:

Questions from text:

Chapter 11: What priest arranged for Joash to be king? ________________

Chapter 12: What did Jehoiada put beside the altar to hold the offerings of the people? ________________________________

Chapter 13: What did Joash, king of Israel, say when weeping over Elisha?

____

____

What does this passage mean?

How does this apply to me?

Messages preached from text:

Questions from text:

Chapter 14: By what prophet did the word of the Lord come? ____________

Chapter 15: Which two kings, does the Bible say, did right in the sight of the Lord? ____________

Chapter 16: Where did Ahaz move the brasen altar? ____________

____

What does this passage mean?

How does this apply to me?

Messages preached from text:

Questions from text:

Chapter 17: Why did the Lord send lions among those that replaced the Israelites in Samaria? ______________________

Chapter 18: What did Hezekiah call the brasen serpent? ______________

What does this passage mean?

How does this apply to me?

Messages preached from text:

Questions from text:

Chapter 19: God said He would defend Jerusalem for whose sake? ________

____

Chapter 20: Why did Isaiah tell Hezekiah, "Set thine house in order?" ____

____

What does this passage mean?

How does this apply to me?

Messages preached from text:

Questions from text:

Chapter 21: What did Manasseh seduce Israel to do? ______________________

____

Chapter 22: Where did they find the book of the law? ____________________

____

What does this passage mean?

How does this apply to me?

Messages preached from text:

Questions from text:

Chapter 23: Which king slew Josiah at Megiddo? ______________________

Chapter 24: Who filled Jerusalem with innocent blood? ________________

Chapter 25: Who did the king of Babylon leave as ruler in the land of Judah?

____

What does this passage mean?

How does this apply to me?

Messages preached from text:

Questions from text:

Chapter 1: Who smote Midian in the field of Moab? ____________________

Chapter 2: Who were the three sons of Zeruiah, David's sister? __________

____

What does this passage mean?

How does this apply to me?

Messages preached from text:

Questions from text:

Chapter 3: How long did David reign in Hebron? ________________
Chapter 4: What four things did Jabez call on God to do? ____________

____

Chapter 5: What were three characteristics of the valiant men of Reuben, Gad, and Manasseh? __________________________

____

What does this passage mean?

How does this apply to me?

Messages preached from text:

Questions from text:

Chapter 6: Who executed the priest's offices in the temple Solomon built?

Chapter 7: How many times does this chapter speak of the sons of Benjamin being "mighty men of valour"? ____________________

What does this passage mean?

How does this apply to me?

Messages preached from text:

Questions from text:

Chapter 8: Where did the "chief men" dwell? ____________________

Chapter 9: Who was called "the seer"? ____________________

Chapter 10: In the battle, by whom was Saul wounded? ____________________

What does this passage mean?

How does this apply to me?

Messages preached from text:

Questions from text:

Chapter 11: Which two men are mentioned to have slain 300? ____________

____

Chapter 12: Upon whom did the spirit come? ____________________

Chatper 13: Against whom was the anger of the Lord kindled? ____________

What does this passage mean?

How does this apply to me?

Messages preached from text:

Questions from text:

Chapter 14: The Lord brought the fear of whom upon all nations? ________

Chapter 15: Who was appointed to sound with cymbals of brass? ________

____

Chapter 16: What three things should we give unto the Lord? ________

____

What does this passage mean?

How does this apply to me?

Messages preached from text:

Questions from text:

Chapter 17: What did the Lord say He would ordain for His people Israel?
Chapter 18: Who slew 18,000 Edomites? ______________________
Chapter 19: Why did David show kindness unto Hanun? ______________

____

Chapter 20: What was the name of David's brother? ______________

What does this passage mean?

How does this apply to me?

Messages preached from text:

Questions from text:

Chapter 21: David said the Lord's____________________ are very great.
Chapter 22: For what did David prepare abundantly before his death? ____
____
Chapter 23: Who was called "the man of God?" ____________________
Chapter 24: Who had "no sons?" __________________________

What does this passage mean?

How does this apply to me?

Messages preached from text:

Questions from text:

Chapter 25: Whose children were under the hands of their father for song in the house of the Lord? ____________________

Chapter 26: Who was "ruler of the treasures?" ____________________

Chapter 27: Whose job was it to be with the king's sons? ____________________

What does this passage mean?

How does this apply to me?

Messages preached from text:

Questions from text:

Chapter 28: Where did David get the pattern for the house of the Lord?

____

Chapter 29: David, speaking to God, said, "____________________ and ____________________ come of thee."

What does this passage mean?

How does this apply to me?

Messages preached from text:

Questions from text:

Chapter 1: What did Solomon make "plenteous" at Jerusalem? __________

____

Chapter 2: Why did Solomon say the house that is to be built must be great?

____

Chapter 3: What was the weight of the nails used for the house? _________

Chapter 4: How many candlesticks did Solomon make for the temple? ____

What does this passage mean?

How does this apply to me?

Messages preached from text:

Questions from text:

Chapter 5: Under what was the ark of the covenant placed? ______________

____

Chapter 6: What did Solomon ask God to remember? ______________

____

What does this passage mean?

How does this apply to me?

Messages preached from text:

Questions from text:

Chapter 7: Why were the people glad and merry in heart? ______________

____

Chapter 8: Whose job was it to praise and minister before the priests?

____

Chapter 9: There "was not ________ ____________ *accounted of in the days of Solomon."*

What does this passage mean?

How does this apply to me?

Messages preached from text:

Questions from text:

Chapter 10: What did the old men tell Rehoboam would happen if he would be kind to the people? ______________________

Chapter 11: Who did Rehoboam have "on his side?" ______________

Chapter 12: When the king and princes humbled themselves, what did they say? ______________________

Chapter 13: What covenant declared that God gave the kingdom of Israel to David? ______________________

What does this passage mean?

How does this apply to me?

Messages preached from text:

Questions from text:

Chapter 14: In the eyes of the Lord, what did Asa do? ______________________

____

Chapter 15: "The Lord is with you, while ye _____ _________ __________."

Chapter 16: Who escaped out of Asa's hand because he did not rely on the Lord? ______________________

Chapter 17: What did Jehoshaphat take away out of Judah? ______________

____

What does this passage mean?

How does this apply to me?

Messages preached from text:

Questions from text:

Chapter 18: Who did God help in this chapter? ______________________
Chapter 19: For what did Jehoshaphat prepare his heart? ______________
Chapter 20: The Spirit of the Lord came upon whom? _________________

What does this passage mean?

How does this apply to me?

Messages preached from text:

Questions from text:

Chapter 21: Elijah said that Jehoram did not walk in the way of which two good kings? ______________________________

Chapter 22: Who destroyed all the seed royal of the house of Judah? ________

Chapter 23: Who anointed Joash king? ______________________

What does this passage mean?

How does this apply to me?

Messages preached from text:

Questions from text:

Chapter 24: Who was a "wicked woman"? ______________________

Chapter 25: What did Joash, king of Israel brake down in Jerusalem? ______

____

Chapter 26: What did King Uzziah love? ______________________

What does this passage mean?

How does this apply to me?

Messages preached from text:

Questions from text:

Chapter 27: What did Jotham not do that his father Uzziah did? ______

______

Chapter 28: Why did the Lord bring Judah low? ______

______

Chapter 29: What prophet is mentioned in this chapter? ______

What does this passage mean?

How does this apply to me?

Messages preached from text:

Questions from text:

Chapter 30: What did Hezekiah tell Israel would happen if they turned again unto the Lord? ____

____

Chapter 31: In what did the priests and Levites sanctify themselves? _______

What does this passage mean?

How does this apply to me?

Messages preached from text:

Questions from text:

Chapter 32: Which two men prayed and cried to God concerning the Assyrians?

____

Chapter 33: Why did Manasseh humble himself greatly? ______________

____

Chapter 34: What did Josiah do in the eighth year of his reign? __________

____

What does this passage mean?

How does this apply to me?

Messages preached from text:

Questions from text:

Chapter 35: What prophet lamented for Josiah? ______________________

Chapter 36: How long would the land of Israel lay desolate? ____________

What does this passage mean?

How does this apply to me?

Messages preached from text:

Questions from text:

Chapter 1: With what did Cyrus ask those who remained to help? ________

____

Chapter 2: Who gave after their ability? ________________

Chapter 3: Why did the returning remnant give meat, drink, and oil to them of Zidon and Tyre? ________________

What does this passage mean?

How does this apply to me?

Messages preached from text:

Questions from text:

Chapter 4: The people of the land____________________ them in building.
Chapter 5: Who helped Zerubbabel and Jeshua begin building the house of God? ____
Chapter 6: For whom did King Darius want the Jews to pray? ____________

What does this passage mean?

How does this apply to me?

Messages preached from text:

Questions from text:

Chapter 7: Ezra came to Jerusalem according to what? ______________________

____

Chapter 8: For what did Ezra proclaim a fast? ______________________

____

What does this passage mean?

How does this apply to me?

Messages preached from text:

Questions from text:

Chapter 9: What did Ezra do when he heard the holy seed had mingled themselves with the people of those lands? ______________________________

Chapter 10: How many days did it take to gather all the men of Judah and Benjamin? ______________________________

What does this passage mean?

How does this apply to me?

Messages preached from text:

Questions from text:

Chapter 1: What does God do for those who love Him and keep His commandments? ______

Chapter 2: What did the king say had not happened before? ______

______

Chapter 3: Who was the "goldsmith's son"? ______

What does this passage mean?

______

______

______

______

______

How does this apply to me?

______

______

______

______

______

______

Messages preached from text:

______

______

______

______

______

______

______

Questions from text:

Chapter 4: What two things did Nehemiah and the people do when they heard their enemies were going to come fight against them? ____________

____

Chapter 5: What did Nehemiah tell the nobles and rulers to "leave off?"

____

Chapter 6: Which prophetess tried to put Nehemiah in fear? ____________

What does this passage mean?

How does this apply to me?

Messages preached from text:

Questions from text:

Chapter 7: Hananiah was known for what two characteristics? ____________

____

Chapter 8: What did Nehemiah say was their strength? ____________

What does this passage mean?

How does this apply to me?

Messages preached from text:

Questions from text:

Chapter 9: Who dealt proudly against Israel? ______________________

____

Chapter 10: To where were the Israelites to bring their firstfruits from the ground and trees? ______________________

Chapter 11: Who was at the king's hand in all matters concerning the people?

____

What does this passage mean?

How does this apply to me?

Messages preached from text:

Questions from text:

Chapter 12: Who was overseer of the singers? ______________________

Chapter 13: Why were the Levites "fled every one to his field?" __________

____

What does this passage mean?

How does this apply to me?

Messages preached from text:

Questions from text:

Chapter 1: To whom did Memucan say Queen Vashti did wrong? ______

______

Chapter 2: What did Esther obtain in the sight of all them that looked upon her? ______

Chapter 3: Who told Haman that Mordecai would not do him reverence?

______

What does this passage mean?

How does this apply to me?

Messages preached from text:

Questions from text:

Chapter 4: What did Mordecai tell Hatach to charge Esther? ______________

Chapter 5: What did the king hold out to Esther the queen? ______________

Chapter 6: Why was Haman come to the outward court of the king's house?

Chapter 7: Where did the king go when he left the banquet in anger?

What does this passage mean?

How does this apply to me?

Messages preached from text:

Questions from text:

Chapter 8: Why did many people of the land become Jews? ______________

____

Chapter 9: To what did the Jews not put their hand? ______________

Chapter 10: What did Mordecai speak to all his seed? ______________

What does this passage mean?

How does this apply to me?

Messages preached from text:

Questions from text:

Chapter 1: How many servants said, "I only am escaped alone to tell thee?"

____

Chapter 2: Job's three friends saw that his ______________ *was very great.*
Chapter 3: Job said life was given to the ______________ *in soul.*
Chapter 4: Why does the old lion perish? ______________
Chapter 5: Unto what is man born? ______________

What does this passage mean?

How does this apply to me?

Messages preached from text:

Questions from text:

Chapter 6: Job said, "ye dig a ______________ for your friend."
Chapter 7: Job said his days were swifter than what? ____________________
Chapter 8: Whose hope shall perish? ______________________________
Chapter 9: Which two persons did Job say God destroyeth alike? ________
____

What does this passage mean?

How does this apply to me?

Messages preached from text:

Questions from text:

Chapter 10: What preserved Job's spirit? ______________________
Chapter 11: Zophar asked Job if his __________ should make men hold their peace.
Chapter 12: With whom is wisdom? ______________________
Chapter 13: Job said, God "shall be my ______________________."
Chapter 14: Job said, "My ______________________ is sealed up in a bag."

What does this passage mean?

How does this apply to me?

Messages preached from text:

Questions from text:

Chapter 15: What shall be the recompence of those who trust in vanity? ____________________

Chapter 16: What did Job say he poured out unto God? ____________________

Chapter 17: What happened to the thoughts of Job's heart? ____________________

Chapter 18: Who was counted as beasts in Job's sight? ____________________

Chapter 19: Who did Job ask to have pity upon him? ____________________

What does this passage mean?

How does this apply to me?

Messages preached from text:

Questions from text:

Chapter 20: Who shall fly away as a dream? ______________________

Chapter 21: Who is "as chaff that the storm carrieth away?" __________

Chapter 22: Who said to Job, "Is not thy wickedness great?" __________

Chapter 23: What does God know? __________________________

What does this passage mean?

How does this apply to me?

Messages preached from text:

Questions from text:

Chapter 24: Of whom does it say "they know not the light?" ______________

Chapter 25: "The stars are not ________________ *in his sight."*

Chapter 26: What did God hang upon nothing? ________________________

Chapter 27: "I will not remove mine _________________________ *from me."*

Chapter 28: From where is iron taken? _____________________________

Chapter 29: What was as a robe and a diadem to Job? __________________

What does this passage mean?

How does this apply to me?

Messages preached from text:

Questions from text:

Chapter 30: What did Job say, "passeth away as a cloud?" ______________

Chapter 31: What did Job say, "was a terror to me?" ______________

____

Chapter 32: "There is a ______________________ *in man."*

Chapter 33: God will render unto man his what? ______________

What does this passage mean?

How does this apply to me?

Messages preached from text:

Questions from text:

Chapter 34: Who drinketh up scorning like water? ____________
Chapter 35: The oppressed cry out by reason of what? ____________
____
Chapter 36: What kind of people "heap up wrath"? ____________
Chapter 37: "By the breath of God ____________ *is given."*
Chapter 38: "The face of the deep is ____________*."*

What does this passage mean?

How does this apply to me?

Messages preached from text:

Questions from text:

Chapter 39: Whose house did God make the wilderness? ______________

Chapter 40: Where did Job say he would lay his hand? ______________

Chapter 41: What did God say was leviathan's pride? ______________

Chapter 42: To which friend of Job did God say His wrath was kindled?

____

What does this passage mean?

How does this apply to me?

Messages preached from text:

Questions from text:

Chapter 1: Whose way shall perish? ____________________

Chapter 2: Who did the psalmist tell to be instructed? ____________

Chapter 3: "Thou, O Lord, art a ____________ *for me."*

Chapter 4: "Put your ____________ *in the Lord."*

Chapter 5: What does God hate? ____________________

Chapter 6: "Oh save me for thy ____________ *sake."*

Chapter 7: Whose mischief will return upon their own head? ________

Chapter 8: Who is man a little lower than? ____________

Chapter 9: What will cause the nations to know themselves to be but men?

____

What does this passage mean?

How does this apply to me?

Messages preached from text:

Questions from text:

Chapter 10: Who did the psalmist ask God not to forget? ____________
Chapter 11: What does God's countenance behold? ____________
Chapter 12: What kind of man ceaseth? ____________
Chapter 13: What did David have in his heart daily? ____________
Chapter 14: What did God look down to see? ____________
____
Chapter 15: What should we speak from our hearts? ____________
Chapter 16: Where did David always set the Lord? ____________
Chapter 17: Who does God use as His hand? ____________
Chapter 18: David was girded with strength for what? ____________

What does this passage mean?

How does this apply to me?

Messages preached from text:

Questions from text:

Chapter 19: What enlightens the eyes? ______________________

Chapter 20: Who will God hear from Heaven? ______________________

Chapter 21: For what did the king ask God? ______________________

Chapter 22: "For the ______________________ is the Lord's."

What does this passage mean?

How does this apply to me?

Messages preached from text:

Questions from text:

Chapter 23: Why do sheep fear no evil? ____________________
Chapter 24: What kind of heart should we have? ____________________
Chapter 25: Who will the Lord "teach his way?" ____________________
Chapter 26: David said, "I shall not slide" because he did what? ____________________
____
Chapter 27: David would faint unless he ____________________.
Chapter 28: "The Lord is my ____________ *and my* ____________."
Chapter 29: With what will the Lord bless His people? ____________________
Chapter 30: What happened to David when God hid His face? ____________________
Chapter 31: Why did David's strength fail? ____________________

What does this passage mean?

How does this apply to me?

Messages preached from text:

Questions from text:

Chapter 32: When shall every one that is godly, pray? ______________________

____

Chapter 33: What two things does the Lord love? ______________________

Chapter 34: Who is the Lord nigh unto? ______________________

Chapter 35: What would David speak of all the day long? ______________________

____

Chapter 36: Where do we see light? ______________________

What does this passage mean?

How does this apply to me?

Messages preached from text:

Questions from text:

Chapter 37: At whom does the Lord laugh? ______________________
Chapter 38: Why did David say there was no rest in his house? ____________
____
Chapter 39: David said his days were as an ______________________.
Chapter 40: What was more than the hairs on David's head? ____________
____
Chapter 41: Who spoke evil of David? ______________________

What does this passage mean?

How does this apply to me?

Messages preached from text:

Questions from text:

Chapter 42: Where did the psalmist go with the multitude? ______________

Chapter 43: What was God to the psalmist's countenance? ______________

Chapter 44: What would God do for His mercies' sake? ______________

Chapter 45: "Thy ______________, O God, is for ever and ever."

Chapter 46: "Come, behold the ______________ of the Lord."

Chapter 47: What did God choose for us? ______________

Chapter 48: What did God use to break the ships of Tarshish? ______________

Chapter 49: How are we laid in the grave? ______________

What does this passage mean?

How does this apply to me?

Messages preached from text:

Questions from text:

Chapter 50: What do the wicked frame in their tongues? ______________
Chapter 51: In what are we conceived? ______________
Chapter 52: What does the man trust in that maketh not God his strength?
____
Chapter 53: When will Jacob rejoice and Israel be glad? ______________
____
Chapter 54: He hath delivered me out of ______________ trouble.
Chapter 55: From what was David delivered in peace? ______________
Chapter 56: How often did they wrest the psalmist's words? ______________

What does this passage mean?

How does this apply to me?

Messages preached from text:

Questions from text:

Chapter 57: "My heart is ______________________, O God"
Chapter 58: Who goes astray as soon as they are born? ____________________
Chapter 59: "God is my ___________________________."
Chapter 60: "God hath spoken in his_____________________________."
Chapter 61: Where did David say he would abide? _________________________
Chapter 62: Trust in God at _______________ times.
Chapter 63: When did David say he would meditate on God? _______________
Chapter 64: Who do the workers of iniquity shoot at in secret? _____________

What does this passage mean?

How does this apply to me?

Messages preached from text:

Questions from text:

Chapter 65: What is full of water? ______________________________
Chapter 66: What did the psalmist say to come and see? ______________

____
Chapter 67: Who shall fear God? ______________________________
Chapter 68: What two things does God give unto His people? __________

____
Chapter 69: Who does the Lord hear? ___________________________

What does this passage mean?

How does this apply to me?

Messages preached from text:

Questions from text:

Chapter 70: The psalmist told God "thou art my________________________."
Chapter 71: What did the psalmist say he would do more and more? ______
____
Chapter 72: God is the only One Who does what? ________________
Chapter 73: What should be the strength of my heart? ____________
Chapter 74: Where do God's enemies roar? ____________________
____
Chapter 75: Whose horn would be exalted? ____________________

What does this passage mean?

How does this apply to me?

Messages preached from text:

Questions from text:

Chapter 76: Where is God's tabernacle? ____________________
Chapter 77: Why could the psalmist not speak? ____________________
Chapter 78: What two things did God do because He was full of compassion? ____________________
Chapter 79: Israel had become a reproach to whom? ____________________

What does this passage mean?

How does this apply to me?

Messages preached from text:

Questions from text:

Chapter 80: The Lord fed whom with the bread of tears? ____________

Chapter 81: What would God do if Israel would hearken unto Him? ____________

Chapter 82: Who will judge the earth? ____________

Chapter 83: "Fill their faces with ____________; that they may seek thy name, O LORD."

Chapter 84: "Blessed is the man whose ____________ is in thee."

Chapter 85: What did the psalmist say he would hear? ____________

Chapter 86: How often did David cry unto the Lord? ____________

Chapter 87: Where did the psalmist say God's foundation was? ____________

What does this passage mean?

How does this apply to me?

Messages preached from text:

Questions from text:

Chapter 88: How often did the psalmist cry before the Lord? ______________

Chapter 89: Of whom did God say, "my covenant shall stand fast with him"?

Chapter 90: "Thou hast set our ________________________ *before thee."*

Chapter 91: Who shall abide under the shadow of the Almighty? __________

Chapter 92: What is a good thing to do? ____________________

What does this passage mean?

How does this apply to me?

Messages preached from text:

Questions from text:

Chapter 93: What is everlasting? ______________________

Chapter 94: When the psalmist's foot slipped, what held him up? ________

____

Chapter 95: What are in the hands of God? ______________________

Chapter 96: Above what is the Lord to be feared? ______________________

Chapter 97: What two things are the habitation of God's throne?

____

Chapter 98: Who should make a "joyful noise"? ______________________

Chapter 99: How many times is the word "holy" used? ______________

Chapter 100: "For the Lord is ______________________*."*

Chapter 101: Who did David want to dwell with him? ______________

What does this passage mean?

How does this apply to me?

Messages preached from text:

Questions from text:

Chapter 102: Whose groaning does the Lord hear? ______________________

Chapter 103: To what two things are man's days compared? ______________

____

Chapter 104: What makes a man's face shine? ______________________

Chapter 105: What two creatures came without number? ______________

____

What does this passage mean?

How does this apply to me?

Messages preached from text:

Questions from text:

Chapter 106: What was a shame to Israel? ______________________
Chapter 107: For what two reasons do men praise the Lord? ______________
____
Chapter 108: Where will God cast His shoe? ______________________
Chapter 109: David said he was tossed up and down like what? __________

What does this passage mean?

How does this apply to me?

Messages preached from text:

Questions from text:

Chapter 110: Who shall the Lord judge? ______________________________

Chapter 111: What is the beginning of wisdom? ________________________

Chapter 112: How long will the righteous be in remembrance? ___________

Chapter 113: Where is the glory of the Lord? __________________________

Chapter 114: What did the Jordan River do at God's presence? __________

____

Chapter 115: What two things was God to Israel, Aaron, and those that fear the Lord? ____

Chapter 116: How long did the psalmist say he would call upon the Lord?

____

Chapter 117: Why should we praise the Lord? _________________________

____

Chapter 118: In what should we rejoice and be glad? __________________

____

What does this passage mean?

How does this apply to me?

Messages preached from text:

Questions from text:

Chapter 119: "The law of thy mouth is better unto me than" what?

What does this passage mean?

How does this apply to me?

Messages preached from text:

Questions from text:

Chapter 120: When did the psalmist cry unto the Lord? ________________

Chapter 121: What did the Lord make? ________________

Chapter 122: For whose sake did David say "Peace be within thee"?

____

Chapter 123: "Have ________________ *upon us."*

Chapter 124: What two things went over our soul? ________________

____

Chapter 125: What abideth forever? ________________

Chapter 126: What is filled with laughter? ________________

Chapter 127: In whose hand are the arrows? ________________

Chapter 128: Who will be an olive plant? ________________

Chapter 129: Although the psalmist was afflicted, what did not happen?

____

Chapter 130: What is "with the Lord"? ________________

What does this passage mean?

How does this apply to me?

Messages preached from text:

Questions from text:

Chapter 131: The psalmist said what was not lofty? ________________

Chapter 132: With what will David clothe the enemies of God? ________

Chapter 133: What descended on the mountain of Zion? ____________

Chapter 134: Where do the servants of the Lord stand? ____________

Chapter 135: Our Lord is above all ______________.

Chapter 136: Who alone does great wonders? ________________

Chapter 137: The Israelites wept when they remembered what? ________

Chapter 138: What did God do on the day David cried? ____________

____

*Chapter 139: "*______________ *me, oh God, and know my heart."*

Chapter 140: What did the proud hide for David? ______________

What does this passage mean?

How does this apply to me?

Messages preached from text:

Questions from text:

Chapter 141: What did David ask the Lord not to keep destitute? ____________
Chapter 142: What did David pour out before the Lord? ____________
Chapter 143: What did David say he would remember? ____________
Chapter 144: What did David say he would sing unto the Lord? ____________
Chapter 145: To whom is the Lord nigh? ____________
Chapter 146: Whose eyes does the Lord open? ____________
Chapter 147: What is good to do? ____________
Chapter 148: Whose name alone is excellent? ____________
Chapter 149: In whom did the psalmist say Israel should rejoice? ____________

____

Chapter 150: Who should praise the Lord? ____________

What does this passage mean?

How does this apply to me?

Messages preached from text:

Questions from text:

Chapter 1: In what do scorners delight? ______________________

Chapter 2: Whose ways are crooked and froward? ______________________

Chapter 3: "Whom the Lord ______________ he correcteth."

Chapter 4: What should be kept with all diligence? ______________________

What does this passage mean?

How does this apply to me?

Messages preached from text:

Questions from text:

Chapter 5: The wicked "shall be holden with" what? ______________________
Chapter 6: What "are the way of life"? ______________________
Chapter 7: To whom should we say, "Thou art my sister"? ______________________
Chapter 8: Those who find wisdom shall obtain what from the Lord? __________
Chapter 9: What are the three descriptions of a foolish woman? __________

____

What does this passage mean?

How does this apply to me?

Messages preached from text:

Questions from text:

Chapter 10: What kind of person will utter a slander? ____________

Chapter 11: "A ____________ revealeth secrets."

Chapter 12: What kind of woman is a crown to her husband? ____________

Chapter 13: "Only by pride cometh ____________."

Chapter 14: "The ____________ believeth every word."

What does this passage mean?

How does this apply to me?

Messages preached from text:

Questions from text:

Chapter 15: What makes a cheerful countenance? ____________________
Chapter 16: Who is an abomination to the Lord? ____________________
Chapter 17: What is the glory of children? ____________________
Chapter 18: What is harder to be won than a strong city? ____________________

____

What does this passage mean?

How does this apply to me?

Messages preached from text:

Questions from text:

Chapter 19: What "are a continual dropping"? ______________________________

____

Chapter 20: What will most men proclaim? ______________________________

Chapter 21: What is more acceptable to the Lord than sacrifice? __________

____

Chapter 22: What will drive foolishness from a child? ____________________

____

Chapter 23: Correction of a child will deliver him from ____________________.

Chapter 24: "A wise man is ______________________________."

What does this passage mean?

How does this apply to me?

Messages preached from text:

Questions from text:

Chapter 25: How is a prince persuaded? ___________________

Chapter 26: Who says, "There is a lion in the way"? ___________________

Chapter 27: A fool's wrath is heavier than what two things? ___________________

What does this passage mean?

How does this apply to me?

Messages preached from text:

Questions from text:

Chapter 28: What kind of men "understand not judgment"? ____________

Chapter 29: What must a king do for his throne to be established forever?

____

Chapter 30: What "is pure"? ____________

Chapter 31: Whose cause should we plead? ____________

What does this passage mean?

How does this apply to me?

Messages preached from text:

Questions from text:

Chapter 1: How many times is the phrase "all is vanity" mentioned? ________

Chapter 2: What does God give to the sinner? ________________________

Chapter 3: Nothing can be put to or taken from what? ________________

____

What does this passage mean?

How does this apply to me?

Messages preached from text:

Questions from text:

Chapter 4: What is not quickly broken? ______________________

Chapter 5: By what is a fool's voice known? ______________________

Chapter 6: The sight of the eyes is better than what? ______________________

Chapter 7: What did Solomon find more bitter than death? ______________________

What does this passage mean?

How does this apply to me?

Messages preached from text:

Questions from text:

Chapter 8: In what war is there no discharge? ____________________

Chapter 9: What is better than a dead lion? ____________________

Chapter 10: We should eat for ______________ *and not for drunkenness.*

Chapter 11: Solomon said to remember the days of ______________.

Chapter 12: What shall return unto God? ____________________

What does this passage mean?

How does this apply to me?

Messages preached from text:

Questions from text:

Chapter 1: Of what does the bride say she was made the keeper? ________

Chapter 2: What do little foxes do? ________

Chapter 3: How many times is the phrase "whom my soul loveth" mentioned?

____

Chapter 4: To what did the bridegroom compare her hair? ________

Chapter 5: How did the bride describe her beloved's eyes? ________

Chapter 6: "My beloved is ________."

Chapter 7: What was described as the fishpools in Heshbon? ________

Chapter 8: What were the keepers of the vineyard to give Solomon for the fruit thereof? ________

What does this passage mean?

How does this apply to me?

Messages preached from text:

Questions from text:

Chapter 1: Who knoweth his owner? ______________________

Chapter 2: What have the house of Jacob made with their own fingers?

____

Chapter 3: With what will God replace well set hair? ______________________

What does this passage mean?

How does this apply to me?

Messages preached from text:

Questions from text:

Chapter 4: The branch of the Lord shall be ___________ and ___________.
Chapter 5: Woe unto them that are wise in what? ___________
Chapter 6: What did Isaiah say when God said, "Whom shall I send?"
____
Chapter 7: What shall every one eat that is left in the land? ___________
____

What does this passage mean?

How does this apply to me?

Messages preached from text:

Questions from text:

Chapter 8: "Should not a people ________________ unto their God?"
Chapter 9: Which two tribes of Israel would be together against Judah?
____

Chapter 10: Who did Isaiah say would return unto the mighty God? ________
____

What does this passage mean?

How does this apply to me?

Messages preached from text:

Questions from text:

Chapter 11: When Christ sets up His kingdom, what will He recover the second time? ______

Chapter 12: "I will trust, and not be ______*."*

Chapter 13: What place would never be inhabited after it was overthrown?

______

Chapter 14: The Lord chose Israel and will set them where? ______

______

Chapter 15: Of what will the waters of Dimon be full? ______

What does this passage mean?

How does this apply to me?

Messages preached from text:

Questions from text:

Chapter 16: Who would be as a wandering bird cast out of the nest? ________

____

Chapter 17: Of what were the children of Israel not mindful? ________

____

Chapter 18: "Whose land the ________ have spoiled."

Chapter 19: What would be called the city of destruction? ________

____

Chapter 20: Isaiah was the son of whom? ________

What does this passage mean?

How does this apply to me?

Messages preached from text:

Questions from text:

Chapter 21: Who was to declare what he seeth? ____________

Chapter 22: What key would be given to God's servant Eliakim? ____________

____

Chapter 23: What would be holiness to the Lord? ____________

____

Chapter 24: What will the Lord empty? ____________

What does this passage mean?

How does this apply to me?

Messages preached from text:

Questions from text:

Chapter 25: God's counsels are _______________ and _________________.
Chapter 26: Where is everlasting strength? ___________________________
Chapter 27: "For it is a people of no ________________________: therefore he that made them will not have mercy on them."
Chapter 28: What will the Lord give to him that sitteth in judgment? ______
____

What does this passage mean?

How does this apply to me?

Messages preached from text:

Questions from text:

Chapter 29: What would happen to the wisdom of the wise men? ________

____

Chapter 30: Whose strength was to sit still? ________________

Chapter 31: The Lord will defend Jerusalem as what? ____________

Chapter 32: Who deviseth wicked devices to destroy the poor? ________

What does this passage mean?

How does this apply to me?

Messages preached from text:

Questions from text:

Chapter 33: What did God say to "acknowledge"? ____________________

Chapter 34: Where will the Lord have a great slaughter? ____________________

____

Chapter 35: When shall waters brake out in the wilderness and streams in the desert? ____________________

Chapter 36: What was like a broken reed? ____________________

What does this passage mean?

How does this apply to me?

Messages preached from text:

Questions from text:

Chapter 37: God said He would defend and save Jerusalem for whose sake?

____

Chapter 38: What sign did the Lord give Hezekiah? ________________

____

Chapter 39: Who told Hezekiah the Word of the Lord? ________________

What does this passage mean?

How does this apply to me?

Messages preached from text:

Questions from text:

Chapter 40: To whom does God give power? ______________________

Chapter 41: With what did God say He would uphold Israel? ______________

____

Chapter 42: To what will God not give His praise? ______________________

What does this passage mean?

How does this apply to me?

Messages preached from text:

Questions from text:

Chapter 43: What did God say He would not remember? ________________

Chapter 44: Who shall not be forgotten of God? ________________

Chapter 45: What things does the Lord declare? ________________

What does this passage mean?

How does this apply to me?

Messages preached from text:

Questions from text:

Chapter 46: God's counsel shall ________________.
Chapter 47: What did God describe as uncovering nakedness? ____________
____
Chapter 48: What was Israel to utter even to the end of the earth? _______
____
Chapter 49: "They shall not be ashamed that ___________________ for me."

What does this passage mean?

How does this apply to me?

Messages preached from text:

Questions from text:

Chapter 50: From what did Jesus not hide His face? ______________________

____

Chapter 51: What did God make to be a light for His people? __________

____

Chapter 52: What would be Israel's rereward? ______________________

Chapter 53: For whom did Jesus make intercession? ______________________

____

What does this passage mean?

How does this apply to me?

Messages preached from text:

Questions from text:

Chapter 54: What was as the waters of Noah to God? ____________________

____

Chapter 55: What does our God abundantly do? ____________________

Chapter 56: "Blessed is the man that doeth" what? ____________________

____

Chapter 57: With whom will the one that inhabiteth eternity dwell? ________

____

Chapter 58: A result of fasting is the glory of the Lord shall be thy ________

____________________________.

What does this passage mean?

How does this apply to me?

Messages preached from text:

Questions from text:

Chapter 59: "The way of ______________________ they know not."
Chapter 60: The nation or kingdom that will not serve Zion will what?
____
Chapter 61: What will God cause to spring forth before all the nations?
____
Chapter 62: Zion (Israel) shall be what in the hand of God? ____________
____

What does this passage mean?

How does this apply to me?

Messages preached from text:

Questions from text:

Chapter 63: What things should we make mention of concerning the Lord?

____

Chapter 64: God meeteth those that what? _______________

Chapter 65: How often did Israel provoke God to anger? _______________

Chapter 66: With whom did God say to rejoice and be glad? _______________

What does this passage mean?

How does this apply to me?

Messages preached from text:

Questions from text:

Chapter 1: Jeremiah was set over the nations to do what six things? ________

Chapter 2: What did God say would correct Israel? ________

Chapter 3: Truly in what is the salvation of Israel? ________

What does this passage mean?

How does this apply to me?

Messages preached from text:

Questions from text:

Chapter 4: God said the whole land would be desolate, but He would not make a full ______________.
Chapter 5: What was one of God's perpetual decrees? ____________________

____

What does this passage mean?

How does this apply to me?

Messages preached from text:

Questions from text:

Chapter 6: Of what was Israel not ashamed? ______________________

____

Chapter 7: In what did God tell Israel not to trust? ______________

Chapter 8: What two reasons were given for Jerusalem's perpetual backsliding? ______________________

What does this passage mean?

How does this apply to me?

Messages preached from text:

Questions from text:

Chapter 9: "Through ___________ they refuse to know me, saith the Lord."
Chapter 10: Why would God scatter the flock of a pastor? _______________
____
Chapter 11: What did Israel do that provoked God to anger? ____________
____

What does this passage mean?

How does this apply to me?

Messages preached from text:

Questions from text:

Chapter 12: "But thou, O Lord, ___________________________ me: thou hast _____________________ me, and _______________ mine heart."
Chapter 13: What two reasons did God give for scattering Judah as stubble in the wind? ____
Chapter 14: What did God say the children of Israel loved to do? _________

What does this passage mean?

How does this apply to me?

Messages preached from text:

Questions from text:

Chapter 15: What had increased to be above the sand of the seas? ______
____

Chapter 16: Who did God say they had done worse than? ______________
____

Chapter 17: What is desperately wicked? ______________________

Chapter 18: God told the men of Judah to return and make their ways and doings ________________.

What does this passage mean?

How does this apply to me?

Messages preached from text:

Questions from text:

Chapter 19: God was going to make Judah and Jerusalem like unto what city? ______________________________

Chapter 20: Who did Jeremiah say mocked him? ______________________________

Chapter 21: God said He would punish Israel according to what? ______________________________

____

What does this passage mean?

How does this apply to me?

Messages preached from text:

Questions from text:

Chapter 22: What king was it "well with" because he judged the cause of the poor and needy? ______

Chapter 23: Who caused Israel to err? ______

Chapter 24: God said to Israel, "I will give them an heart to ______ me."

What does this passage mean?

How does this apply to me?

Messages preached from text:

Questions from text:

Chapter 25: To what did the Lord say He would give the wicked? ___________

Chapter 26: Whose hand was with Jeremiah to help him? ___________

Chapter 27: What would happen to the nation that would not put their neck under the yoke of the king of Babylon? ___________

What does this passage mean?

How does this apply to me?

Messages preached from text:

Questions from text:

Chapter 28: How would they know if the Lord had truly sent the prophet?

____

Chapter 29: What priest read a letter to Jeremiah? ____________________

Chapter 30: "Thy bruise is ____________, and thy wound is ____________."

What does this passage mean?

How does this apply to me?

Messages preached from text:

Questions from text:

Chapter 31: With what did God draw Israel to Him? ____________________
Chapter 32: What has God made by His great power and stretched-out arm?

____

What does this passage mean?

How does this apply to me?

Messages preached from text:

Questions from text:

Chapter 33: What cannot be numbered? ______________________

Chapter 34: Who would God cause to return to Jerusalem and fight against it? ______________________

What does this passage mean?

How does this apply to me?

Messages preached from text:

Questions from text:

Chapter 35: Who did the Lord send to Israel? ______________________

____

Chapter 36: What did Baruch write down from the mouth of Jeremiah?

____

Chapter 37: In what did the Lord say, "Deceive not yourselves"? __________

____

What does this passage mean?

How does this apply to me?

Messages preached from text:

Questions from text:

Chapter 38: How many men did Ebed-melech take with him to take Jeremiah out of the dungeon? ______________________________

Chapter 39: Who did Nebuzar-adan the captain of the guard leave in the land of Judah? ______________________________

Chapter 40: Who thought Johanan the son of Kareah spake falsely? ______
____

What does this passage mean?

How does this apply to me?

Messages preached from text:

Questions from text:

Chapter 41: How many men did Ishmael take with him when he smote Gedaliah? ____________________

Chapter 42: "For ye ____________ *in your hearts, when ye sent me unto the Lord your God."*

Chapter 43: Who did the Lord refer to as "my servant"? ____________

What does this passage mean?

How does this apply to me?

Messages preached from text:

Questions from text:

Chapter 44: What did God say would happen to "all the men of Judah that are in the land of Egypt"? ______________________________

____

Chapter 45: What did Baruch say he could not find? ______________

Chapter 46: Why were Egypt's valiant men swept away? ______________

____

Chapter 47: Who did Jeremiah prophesy that the Lord would spoil? ________

____

What does this passage mean?

How does this apply to me?

Messages preached from text:

Questions from text:

Chapter 48: Which two things did Moab trust in that caused them to be taken and destroyed? ______________________________

Chapter 49: Who did God say He would preserve alive? ______________

____

What does this passage mean?

How does this apply to me?

Messages preached from text:

Questions from text:

Chapter 50: "Israel is a ____________________ sheep."

What does this passage mean?

How does this apply to me?

Messages preached from text:

Questions from text:

Chapter 51: What did God say He would do upon the graven images of Babylon? ______________________________

Chapter 52: Who did evil in the eyes of the Lord? ______________________________

What does this passage mean?

How does this apply to me?

Messages preached from text:

Questions from text:

Chapter 1: What did the people give for meat to relieve their soul? ________

____

Chapter 2: What was "no more"? ________________________________

What does this passage mean?

How does this apply to me?

Messages preached from text:

Questions from text:

Chapter 3: Of what does the Lord not approve? ______________________

____

Chapter 4: The Israelites watched for a nation that could not what? ______

____

Chapter 5: What did they want the Lord to consider and behold? ________

____

What does this passage mean?

How does this apply to me?

Messages preached from text:

Questions from text:

Chapter 1: The appearance of the likeness of the glory of the Lord was as what? ______________________________

Chapter 2: What was mentioned in the roll of the book? ______________________________

____

Chapter 3: The roll in Ezekiel's mouth was as what? ______________________________

____

What does this passage mean?

How does this apply to me?

Messages preached from text:

Questions from text:

Chapter 4: Why would Jerusalem be in want for bread and water? ________

____

Chapter 5: What did Israel do that caused God to diminish them and not have any pity? ____

Chapter 6: What phrase is mentioned four times? ____________________

____

Chapter 7: What was the stumblingblock of Israel's iniquity? ____________

____

What does this passage mean?

How does this apply to me?

Messages preached from text:

Questions from text:

Chapter 8: What abominations were men doing at the temple? ____________

____

Chapter 9: The iniquity of the house of Israel is exceeding ____________.

Chapter 10: What did the cherubim wings sound like? ____________

____

Chapter 11: What did God say "I know" about Israel? ____________

____

What does this passage mean?

How does this apply to me?

Messages preached from text:

Questions from text:

Chapter 12: There shall be no more any ________________ vision nor ________________________ divination within the house of Israel.

Chapter 13: What were the prophets of Israel like? ____________________

____

Chapter 14: "Thus saith the Lord God; __________________________ and ________________________ yourselves from your idols."

Chapter 15: What did the Lord call Ezekiel? _________________________

What does this passage mean?

How does this apply to me?

Messages preached from text:

Questions from text:

Chapter 16: What proverb would be used against Jerusalem? ______________

____

Chapter 17: What did the Lord tell Ezekiel to put forth unto the house of Israel? ______________________________

What does this passage mean?

How does this apply to me?

Messages preached from text:

Questions from text:

Chapter 18: What should we do so that iniquity is not our ruin? ____________

____

Chapter 19: What did the whelps that became young lions learn? ____________

____

Chapter 20: Whose hand was lifted up against Israel? ____________

____

What does this passage mean?

How does this apply to me?

Messages preached from text:

Questions from text:

Chapter 21: Why was Ezekiel to cry and howl? ______________________

____

Chapter 22: Israel's princes are like what? ______________________

What does this passage mean?

How does this apply to me?

Messages preached from text:

Questions from text:

Chapter 23: What had Jerusalem played in her youth? __________
Chapter 24: When would Ezekiel be more dumb? __________

What does this passage mean?

How does this apply to me?

Messages preached from text:

Questions from text:

Chapter 25: What did God say He would make Rabbah? ____________

____

Chapter 26: What would Tyrus become to the nations? ____________

Chapter 27: From what did Tyrus make the sails for their ships? ____________

____

What does this passage mean?

How does this apply to me?

Messages preached from text:

Questions from text:

Chapter 28: Who is referred to as being in Eden, the garden of God? ______

______

Chapter 29: What would be the wages for Nebuchadrezzar's army? ______

______

Chapter 30: What would happen to all of Egypt's helpers? ______

______

What does this passage mean?

How does this apply to me?

Messages preached from text:

Questions from text:

Chapter 31: Who was compared to a cedar of Lebanon? ________________
Chapter 32: Who was like a whale in the sea? ________________
Chapter 33: "For with their mouth they shew much ________________, but their heart goeth after their ________________."

What does this passage mean?

How does this apply to me?

Messages preached from text:

Questions from text:

Chapter 34: With what two things did the shepherds rule the sheep? ______

Chapter 35: When will the Lord make Mount Seir desolate? ______

What does this passage mean?

How does this apply to me?

Messages preached from text:

Questions from text:

Chapter 36: "I will put my spirit within you and cause you to walk in" what?

Chapter 37: The Lord will take the children of Israel from among whom?

Chapter 38: The Lord said He was against whom? ______________________

What does this passage mean?

How does this apply to me?

Messages preached from text:

Questions from text:

Chapter 39: God said He would pour out His Spirit upon whom? ____________

____

Chapter 40: How long was every little chamber? ____________

What does this passage mean?

How does this apply to me?

Messages preached from text:

Questions from text:

Chapter 41: What is the table of the Lord? ____________________

Chapter 42: With what did the man measure? ____________________

Chapter 43: What filled the house? ____________________

What does this passage mean?

How does this apply to me?

Messages preached from text:

Questions from text:

Chapter 44: Who kept the charge of God's sanctuary? ______________

____

Chapter 45: What were they to use to cleanse the sanctuary? ______________

____

What does this passage mean?

How does this apply to me?

Messages preached from text:

Questions from text:

Chapter 46: "But the gate shall not be shut until the ________________."
Chapter 47: Of the twelve tribes of Israel, who would have two portions?

____

Chapter 48: In what verse does it say "the sanctuary of the house shall be in the midst thereof"? ________________________________

What does this passage mean?

How does this apply to me?

Messages preached from text:

Questions from text:

Chapter 1: Who did the prince of the eunuchs set over Daniel, Hananiah, Mishael, and Azariah? ____________________

Chapter 2: To whom does God give knowledge? ____________________

____

What does this passage mean?

How does this apply to me?

Messages preached from text:

Questions from text:

Chapter 3: How many more times did Nebuchadnezzar heat the furnace up before casting the Hebrew children into the fire? ____________________

Chapter 4: By what did Nebuchadnezzar think he built the kingdom?

____

What does this passage mean?

How does this apply to me?

Messages preached from text:

Questions from text:

Chapter 5: Who humbled not his heart? ______________________

Chapter 6: How long was every man not to ask a petition of any God or man?
____

Chapter 7: What was the second beast like? ______________________

What does this passage mean?

How does this apply to me?

Messages preached from text:

Questions from text:

Chapter 8: What represented the kings of Media and Persia in the vision?

____

Chapter 9: To whom does righteousness belong? ____________________

What does this passage mean?

How does this apply to me?

Messages preached from text:

Questions from text:

Chapter 10: Daniel was shown that which is noted in the ______________ of truth.

Chapter 11: What kind of people will be strong and do exploits? __________

____

Chapter 12: What shall the wicked do? ______________________

What does this passage mean?

How does this apply to me?

Messages preached from text:

Questions from text:

Chapter 1: By whom would God save the house of Judah? ______________

Chapter 2: What names would God take away out of Israel's mouth? ______________

Chapter 3: Afterward Israel will return and do what? ______________

Chapter 4: Upon what did Israel set their heart? ______________

Chapter 5: What day shall Ephraim be desolate? ______________

Chapter 6: "Come and let us ______________ *unto the LORD."*

Chapter 7: Ephraim did not cry unto the Lord with what? ______________

What does this passage mean?

How does this apply to me?

Messages preached from text:

Questions from text:

Chapter 8: "For they have sown the wind, and they shall reap the ______ ______."

Chapter 9: Why would God cast Ephraim away? ______

Chapter 10: Who is as an heifer that is taught? ______

Chapter 11: Who yet ruleth with God, and is faithful with the saints? ______

Chapter 12: What was used by the ministry of the prophets? ______

Chapter 13: Why did Samaria become desolate? ______

Chapter 14: How would God love Israel? ______

What does this passage mean?

How does this apply to me?

Messages preached from text:

Questions from text:

Chapter 1: Where should the elders and all the inhabitants of the land be gathered? ______________________

Chapter 2: What will the Lord pour out upon all flesh? ______________

Chapter 3: For what will the Lord plead? ______________________

____

What does this passage mean?

How does this apply to me?

Messages preached from text:

Questions from text:

Chapter 1: How many times is the word "transgressions" used? ________

Chapter 2: God raised up Israel's son for what? ________

Chapter 3: What does God reveal to His servants, the prophets? ________

____

Chapter 4: How many times does God say to Israel, "Yet have ye not returned unto me"? ________

Chapter 5: "Seek the ________, *and ye shall live."*

What does this passage mean?

How does this apply to me?

Messages preached from text:

Questions from text:

Chapter 6: Into what did Israel turn judgment? ________________
Chapter 7: Where did Amaziah tell Amos to go? ________________
Chapter 8: What did Amos see? ________________
Chapter 9: The day is come when the plowman shall overtake whom?
____

What does this passage mean?

How does this apply to me?

Messages preached from text:

Questions from text:

Obadiah: "As thou hast ________________, it shall be done unto thee."
Chapter 1: Who asked Jonah, "What meanest thou, O sleeper?" ________
____
Chapter 2: What compassed Jonah about? ____________________
Chapter 3: How long should it have taken Jonah to get to Nineveh? ______
Chapter 4: What did God use to smite the gourd? ______________

What does this passage mean?

How does this apply to me?

Messages preached from text:

Questions from text:

Chapter 1: Of whom is it said, "the transgressions of Israel were found in thee"? ____________________

Chapter 2: "Woe to them that devise ____________________*."*

Chapter 3: The prophets of Jerusalem divine for what? ____________________

Chapter 4: Where would the Lord redeem Israel from their enemies? ________

Chapter 5: Who would be like a lion among the beasts of the forest? ________

____

Chapter 6: Israel would eat, but not be ____________________*.*

Chapter 7: In what does God delight? ____________________

What does this passage mean?

How does this apply to me?

Messages preached from text:

Questions from text:

Chapter 1: The Lord knoweth them that what? ______________
Chapter 2: Who would be led away captive? ______________
Chapter 3: All of Nineveh's strong holds would be like what? ______________

What does this passage mean?

How does this apply to me?

Messages preached from text:

Questions from text:

Chapter 1: To whom did the Chaldeans impute power? ____________________
Chapter 2: "Woe to him that ____________________ *that which is not his!"*
Chapter 3: "The Lord God is my ____________________*."*

What does this passage mean?

How does this apply to me?

Messages preached from text:

Questions from text:

Chapter 1: Who would cry bitterly in the day of the Lord? ______________

Chapter 2: What people did God say He would destroy that there be no inhabitant? ______________________________________

Chapter 3: Of whom did the Lord say, "He will rejoice over thee with joy"?

____

What does this passage mean?

How does this apply to me?

Messages preached from text:

Questions from text:

Chapter 1: Who is called "the LORD'S messenger"? ______________________

Chapter 2: What did God say, "I will fill with glory"? ______________________

What does this passage mean?

How does this apply to me?

Messages preached from text:

Questions from text:

Chapter 1: For whom was the Lord jealous? ______________________

Chapter 2: "He that toucheth __________ *toucheth the apple of his eye."*

Chapter 3: The Lord told Joshua that "if" he did what two things "then" he would judge his house? ______________________

Chapter 4: "Not by might, nor by power, but by my __________________*."*

Chapter 5: What were the dimensions of the flying roll? ______________

____

What does this passage mean?

How does this apply to me?

Messages preached from text:

Questions from text:

Chapter 6: What did the angel say the four horses represented? ____________

____

Chapter 7: Which four people did the Lord tell them not to oppress? ______

____

Chapter 8: Who will come one day to seek the Lord in Jerusalem and pray before the Lord? ____________

Chapter 9: What country shall be devoured by fire? ____________

Chapter 10: They were troubled because there was no what? ____________

What does this passage mean?

How does this apply to me?

Messages preached from text:

Questions from text:

Chapter 11: What kind of shepherd "leaveth" the flock? ________________

Chapter 12: "They shall look upon me whom they have ________________*."*

Chapter 13: In that day what two things will the Lord cause to pass out of the land? ________________

Chapter 14: What shall be upon the bells of the horses? ________________

____

What does this passage mean?

How does this apply to me?

Messages preached from text:

Questions from text:

Chapter 1: What people does the Lord have indignation against forever?

____

Chapter 2: God cursed the priests because they did what with His warning?

____

Chapter 3: What two things will the Lord be like at His coming? __________

____

Chapter 4: Who shall the Lord not leave "root nor branch"? __________

What does this passage mean?

How does this apply to me?

Messages preached from text:

Questions from text:

Chapter 1: Joseph was "a ____________________ man."
Chapter 2: Did the wise men come to a manger or a house to see Jesus?
____
Chapter 3: Who did John call a "generation of vipers"? ____________
Chapter 4: What did Jesus hear before He departed into Galilee? ________
____

What does this passage mean?

How does this apply to me?

Messages preached from text:

Questions from text:

Chapter 5: How far are you to go with "whosoever shall compel thee to go a mile"? ______________________

Chapter 6: "Ye cannot serve God and ______________________."

What does this passage mean?

How does this apply to me?

Messages preached from text:

Questions from text:

Chapter 7: What can a good tree not bring forth? ______________________

Chapter 8: Who said, "I am not worthy"? ______________________

Chapter 9: What made the woman with an issue of blood whole? __________

____

What does this passage mean?

How does this apply to me?

Messages preached from text:

Questions from text:

Chapter 10: Whose surname was Thaddaeus? ______________________

Chapter 11: To whom did Jesus say if they came to Him He would give them rest? ______________________

Chapter 12: What did Jesus say, "shall not be forgiven him?" ______________________

What does this passage mean?

How does this apply to me?

Messages preached from text:

Questions from text:

Chapter 13: Why did Jesus not do many mighty works in Nazareth? ________

Chapter 14: How many baskets full of fragments were left after feeding the 5,000? ________

What does this passage mean?

How does this apply to me?

Messages preached from text:

Questions from text:

Chapter 15: How many men did Jesus feed with seven loaves and a few fish?

Chapter 16: Who said that Jesus was "the Christ,the Son of the living God?"

Chapter 17: "Nothing shall be impossible unto you," if ye have what?

What does this passage mean?

How does this apply to me?

Messages preached from text:

Questions from text:

Chapter 18: "If thy brother shall trespass against thee," what should you go and do? ______________________________

Chapter 19: What should man not put asunder? ______________________________

____

Chapter 20: Against whom did the labourers in the vineyard murmur? ______

____

What does this passage mean?

How does this apply to me?

Messages preached from text:

Questions from text:

Chapter 21: The people took Jesus for a ______________________.
Chapter 22: What is the greatest commandment? ____________________
____

What does this passage mean?

How does this apply to me?

Messages preached from text:

Questions from text:

Chapter 23: Who did Jesus say "shall be exalted"? ______________________

____

Chapter 24: To whom is Jesus speaking in chapter 24? ______________________

What does this passage mean?

How does this apply to me?

Messages preached from text:

Questions from text:

Chapter 25: What has God prepared for the saved since the foundation of the world? ______

Chapter 26: What did the disciples say when Jesus said, "one of you shall betray me"? ______

What does this passage mean?

How does this apply to me?

Messages preached from text:

Questions from text:

Chapter 27: What man of Cyrene did the soldiers compel to bear Jesus' cross? ______

Chapter 28: What happened to the earth when the angel rolled back the stone? ______

What does this passage mean?

How does this apply to me?

Messages preached from text:

Questions from text:

Chapter 1: In what type of "place" did Jesus pray? ______________________

Chapter 2: What was "made for man"? ______________________

Chapter 3: Who did Jesus say "is my brother, and my sister, and mother"?

____

What does this passage mean?

How does this apply to me?

Messages preached from text:

Questions from text:

Chapter 4: What three things "choke the word?" ______________________

____

Chapter 5: How long did the woman have an issue of blood before she was healed? ______________________

What does this passage mean?

How does this apply to me?

Messages preached from text:

Questions from text:

Chapter 6: Why was Jesus moved with compassion toward the people?

Chapter 7: The Pharisees found fault with Jesus' disciples about what?

What does this passage mean?

How does this apply to me?

Messages preached from text:

Questions from text:

Chapter 8: To whom did Jesus say, "Get thee behind me?" ______________

Chapter 9: Why did Jesus say the disciples could not cast out the foul spirit?

____

What does this passage mean?

How does this apply to me?

Messages preached from text:

Questions from text:

Chapter 10: "Whosoever will be ________________ *among you, shall be your* ____________________."

Chapter 11: What two things should you do in order to get what you desire?
____

Chapter 12: What are we to render unto God? ________________________

What does this passage mean?

How does this apply to me?

Messages preached from text:

Questions from text:

Chapter 13: What was spoken of by Daniel the prophet? __________

Chapter 14: With whom was Peter sitting in the palace of the high priest?

What does this passage mean?

How does this apply to me?

Messages preached from text:

Questions from text:

Chapter 15: Who was an honourable counselor? ______________________

Chapter 16: Out of whom did Jesus cast seven devils? ______________________

____

What does this passage mean?

How does this apply to me?

Messages preached from text:

Questions from text:

Chapter 1: Why was Zacharias made dumb (not able to speak)? ________

____

What does this passage mean?

How does this apply to me?

Messages preached from text:

Questions from text:

Chapter 2: Where did Joseph and Mary find Jesus after looking for him for three days? ____________________

Chapter 3: "The axe is laid unto the ____________________ *of the trees."*

What does this passage mean?

How does this apply to me?

Messages preached from text:

Questions from text:

Chapter 4: What did Jesus say "I must" do? ____________________
Chapter 5: For whom did Jesus come to call to repentance? __________
Chapter 6: What should we be that our Father is also? ______________

What does this passage mean?

How does this apply to me?

Messages preached from text:

Questions from text:

Chapter 7: Who said, "I am not worthy?" ______________________

What does this passage mean?

How does this apply to me?

Messages preached from text:

Questions from text:

Chapter 8: The man out of whom the devils were departed was told to return home to do what? ______________________________

Chapter 9: Who did Jesus say "shall be great?" ______________________

What does this passage mean?

How does this apply to me?

Messages preached from text:

Questions from text:

Chapter 10: Which two people saw the wounded man and "passed by on the other side"? ______________________

Chapter 11: Who made clean the outside of the cup, when the inward part was full of wickedness? ______________________

What does this passage mean?

How does this apply to me?

Messages preached from text:

Questions from text:

Chapter 12: After what things do the nations of the world seek? ___________

___

Chapter 13: Which two verses are mentioned identically in the passage? ___

What does this passage mean?

How does this apply to me?

Messages preached from text:

Questions from text:

Chapter 14: What will happen to the man that humbleth himself? ________

____

Chapter 15: "There is joy in the presence of the ________________ *of God over one sinner that repenteth."*

What does this passage mean?

How does this apply to me?

Messages preached from text:

Questions from text:

Chapter 16: Who will be faithful in much? ______________________________
Chapter 17: The leper, who turned back, did what with a loud voice? ______

____

Chapter 18: What shall a person receive in this present time for leaving house, parents, brethren, wife, or children for the kingdom of God's sake?

____

What does this passage mean?

How does this apply to me?

Messages preached from text:

Questions from text:

Chapter 19: What would cry out if the multitude of the disciples had not praised Jesus? ______________________

Chapter 20: What did the Sadducees deny? ______________________

What does this passage mean?

How does this apply to me?

Messages preached from text:

Questions from text:

Chapter 21: What two things shall pass away? ______________________

Chapter 22: What did Peter do after he denied Christ the third time? ______

____

What does this passage mean?

How does this apply to me?

Messages preached from text:

Questions from text:

Chapter 23: What did the centurion say after Jesus died? ______________

____

Chapter 24: What happened to Jesus when Cleopas realized He was Christ?

____

What does this passage mean?

How does this apply to me?

Messages preached from text:

Questions from text:

Chapter 1: Who brought his brother to Jesus? ________________________

Chapter 2: Jesus told those who sold in the temple not to make "my Father's house an house of __________________________*."*

Chapter 3: What Old Testament story was used to illustrate Jesus being lifted up on the cross? ______________________________________

What does this passage mean?

How does this apply to me?

Messages preached from text:

Questions from text:

Chapter 4: What kind of water did Jesus offer the woman at the well?

Chapter 5: Whose writings did Jesus repeat that the Jews did not believe?

What does this passage mean?

How does this apply to me?

Messages preached from text:

Questions from text:

Chapter 6: Why did the Jews murmur against Jesus? ______________________

____

What does this passage mean?

How does this apply to me?

Messages preached from text:

Questions from text:

Chapter 7: Why was the Holy Ghost not yet given? ____________________

____

Chapter 8: Who did Jesus say was a murderer and a liar? ____________

What does this passage mean?

How does this apply to me?

Messages preached from text:

Questions from text:

Chapter 9: What does the word "Siloam" mean? ____________________
Chapter 10: It was said of Jesus that all things John spake of Him were ___
________________.

What does this passage mean?

How does this apply to me?

Messages preached from text:

Questions from text:

Chapter 11: Who did Jesus refer to as "our friend"? ______________________
Chapter 12: Why did many of the chief rulers that believed, not confess Jesus? ______________________
Chapter 13: What was the "new commandment" that Jesus gave His disciples?
____

What does this passage mean?

How does this apply to me?

Messages preached from text:

Questions from text:

Chapter 14: To whom did Jesus say He would manifest Himself? ____________

____

Chapter 15: For what did Jesus say, "I have chosen you, and ordained you"?

____

Chapter 16: "...In me ye might have ____________________."

What does this passage mean?

How does this apply to me?

Messages preached from text:

Questions from text:

Chapter 17: To where did Jesus send His disciples and us? ______________

Chapter 18: What happened to the officers that came to take Jesus when He said, "I am He?" ______________________________

What does this passage mean?

How does this apply to me?

Messages preached from text:

Questions from text:

Chapter 19: What did they give Jesus to drink when He said "I thirst"?

____

Chapter 20: What did Jesus say when He breathed on His disciples?

____

Chapter 21: How many times did Jesus show Himself to the disciples after He had risen from the dead? ______________________

What does this passage mean?

How does this apply to me?

Messages preached from text:

Questions from text:

Chapter 1: What Old Testament character had spoken before concerning Judas? ______________________

Chapter 2: What hour of the day did Peter preach to the people? ________

Chapter 3: What was the name of the porch the people ran to, in order to see the lame man that was healed? ______________________

What does this passage mean?

How does this apply to me?

Messages preached from text:

Questions from text:

Chapter 4: "The multitude of them that believed were of one ____________ and of one _________________."

Chapter 5: "We ought to obey ____________ rather than _____________."

Chapter 6: How many men did they choose to serve tables? _____________

What does this passage mean?

How does this apply to me?

Messages preached from text:

Questions from text:

Chapter 7: Those who stoned Stephen laid their clothes down at whose feet?

____

Chapter 8: Who carried Stephen to his burial? ______________________

What does this passage mean?

How does this apply to me?

Messages preached from text:

Questions from text:

Chapter 9: Who brought Saul to the apostles at Jerusalem? ____________

Chapter 10: What did the voice tell Peter not to call "common"? ________

____

What does this passage mean?

How does this apply to me?

Messages preached from text:

Questions from text:

Chapter 11: Barnabas exhorted that with purpose of heart they would what?

____

Chapter 12: Who did Herod kill with the sword? ________________

What does this passage mean?

How does this apply to me?

Messages preached from text:

Questions from text:

Chapter 13: Who did Paul call a child of the devil? ______________________

Chapter 14: What did Paul preach in the cities of Lycaonia? _____________

Chapter 15: Who was considered "chief men among the brethren"? _______

____

What does this passage mean?

How does this apply to me?

Messages preached from text:

Questions from text:

Chapter 16: Who heard Paul and Silas pray and sing praises? ______________

Chapter 17: The men of Athens had an altar with what inscription? ________

____

Chapter 18: Who was the deputy of Achaia? ____________________

What does this passage mean?

How does this apply to me?

Messages preached from text:

Questions from text:

Chapter 19: The people of Ephesus worshipped what false goddess? ________

____

Chapter 20: From what did Paul say he was pure? ________

What does this passage mean?

How does this apply to me?

Messages preached from text:

Questions from text:

Chapter 21: How many daughters did Philip have? ____________________
Chapter 22: Paul was brought up at the feet of whom? ________________
Chapter 23: How many made a conspiracy to kill Paul? ________________

What does this passage mean?

How does this apply to me?

Messages preached from text:

Questions from text:

Chapter 24: What was the name of the chief captain? ____________________
Chapter 25: What is another name for Augustus? ____________________
Chapter 26: Festus said to Paul, "much learning doth make thee ________."

What does this passage mean?

How does this apply to me?

Messages preached from text:

Questions from text:

Chapter 27: How many people were on the ship? ____________________

Chapter 28: What two things did Paul use to persuade the Jews at Rome?

____

What does this passage mean?

How does this apply to me?

Messages preached from text:

Questions from text:

Chapter 1: God gives the ungodly "up" to what two things? ______________

____

Chapter 2: God will render to every man according to what? ______________

Chapter 3: All the world is ______________ *before God.*

Chapter 4: Jesus was delivered for our ______________ *and raised again for our* ______________.

What does this passage mean?

How does this apply to me?

Messages preached from text:

Questions from text:

Chapter 5: For whom did Christ die in due time? ____________________
Chapter 6: We are buried with Christ by what? ____________________
Chapter 7: How many times does this chapter say "sin that dwelleth in me"?
____
Chapter 8: Walk not after the ______________ *but after the* ____________.

What does this passage mean?

How does this apply to me?

Messages preached from text:

Questions from text:

Chapter 9: What two types of "vessels" are mentioned in the chapter?

____

Chapter 10: For whom did Paul pray, that they might be saved? __________

Chapter 11: Paul said, "I am the apostle of the __________________."

What does this passage mean?

How does this apply to me?

Messages preached from text:

Questions from text:

Chapter 12: How should one show mercy? ____________________
Chapter 13: To whom are rulers a terror? ____________________
Chapter 14: To whom does a servant stand or fall? ____________________
Chapter 15: Who "pleased not himself"? ____________________
Chapter 16: Who had a church in their house? ____________________

What does this passage mean?

How does this apply to me?

Messages preached from text:

Questions from text:

Chapter 1: "He that ______________, let him glory in the__________."
Chapter 2: What was Paul determined to know? ______________________
Chapter 3: Let no man glory in _____________.
Chapter 4: Who was made a spectacle unto the world? ____________
Chapter 5: What two sins are paralleled with leaven? ______________
____

What does this passage mean?

How does this apply to me?

Messages preached from text:

Questions from text:

Chapter 6: With what two things should we glorify God? ________________

Chapter 7: If an unbelieving partner departs, what should you do? ________

____

Chapter 8: Who is known of God? ______________________________

Chapter 9: "Every man that striveth for the mastery is ________________ *in all things."*

What does this passage mean?

How does this apply to me?

Messages preached from text:

Questions from text:

Chapter 10: Why did God destroy some with serpents? ____________

____

*Chapter 11: What does nature teach us?*____________

____

Chapter 12: If one member suffers, what do the rest do? ____________

____

Chapter 13: What does charity not seek? ____________

What does this passage mean?

How does this apply to me?

Messages preached from text:

Questions from text:

Chapter 14: "Let all things be done unto ______________________."

Chapter 15: What are the four kinds of flesh that Paul named? ____________

____

Chapter 16: Who worked the work of the Lord like Apostle Paul? __________

What does this passage mean?

How does this apply to me?

Messages preached from text:

Questions from text:

Chapter 1: "We should not trust in ______________, but in ______."
Chapter 2: Who causeth us to triumph in Christ? ________________________
Chapter 3: What did Paul say was "known and read of all men"? __________
____
Chapter 4: The things which are not seen are __________________.
Chapter 5: "They which live should not henceforth live unto ______________, but unto ______________ which died for them."

What does this passage mean?

How does this apply to me?

Messages preached from text:

Questions from text:

Chapter 6: Why should we give no offence in any thing? ______________

____

Chapter 7: Who did the church of Corinth receive with fear and trembling?

____

Chapter 8: Who was rich, but became poor, that we might be rich? ______

Chapter 9: What was God able to make abound toward you? ______________

What does this passage mean?

How does this apply to me?

Messages preached from text:

Questions from text:

Chapter 10: "He that glorieth, let him glory in the ______________."
Chapter 11: What did Paul say, "cometh upon me daily"? ______________
____
Chapter 12: What verse says, "I love you"? ______________
Chapter 13: "In the mouth of two or three witnesses shall every word be ______________."

What does this passage mean?

How does this apply to me?

Messages preached from text:

Questions from text:

Chapter 1: Paul's reputation went from "he that persecuted us" to what?

____

Chapter 2: "God accepteth no man's ______________________."

Chapter 3: What hath the scripture concluded? ______________________

What does this passage mean?

How does this apply to me?

Messages preached from text:

Questions from text:

Chapter 4: What happened "when the fullness of time was come"?

Chapter 5: Someone hindered the Galatians from doing what daily?

Chapter 6: Unto whom should we "especially" do good?

What does this passage mean?

How does this apply to me?

Messages preached from text:

Questions from text:

Chapter 1: "We should be _________ and without __________ before Him."
Chapter 2: Who is "our peace"? ______________________________________
Chapter 3: We should be rooted and grounded in what? _________________

What does this passage mean?

How does this apply to me?

Messages preached from text:

Questions from text:

Chapter 4: We should "put on" what? ______________________

Chapter 5: With what does God sanctify and cleanse the church? ________

____

Chapter 6: What shall a man receive of the Lord whether he be bond or free?

____

What does this passage mean?

How does this apply to me?

Messages preached from text:

Questions from text:

Chapter 1: What did Paul pray would abound more and more? ____________

Chapter 2: "Let nothing be done through __________ *or* ________________."

Chapter 3: Paul had no confidence in the ____________________.

Chapter 4: Who did Paul beseech to be of the same mind? ______________

____

What does this passage mean?

How does this apply to me?

Messages preached from text:

Questions from text:

Chapter 1: We made peace with God through what? ____________________

Chapter 2: In what one thing did Paul say, "Let no man judge you"? ______

Chapter 3: Above all things we should put on what? ____________________

Chapter 4: In what should we continue? ____________________

What does this passage mean?

How does this apply to me?

Messages preached from text:

Questions from text:

Chapter 1: Who delivers from the wrath to come? ____________________

Chapter 2: Where was Paul shamefully entreated? ____________________

Chapter 3: Of what did Paul say, "we are appointed thereunto"? __________

Chapter 4: Of what did Paul say, "ye need not that I write unto you"? _____

____

Chapter 5: Paul said not to sleep as do others, but to ____________________ *and be* ____________________.

What does this passage mean?

How does this apply to me?

Messages preached from text:

Questions from text:

Chapter 1: What did Paul tell the church "aboundeth" (increaseth) toward each other? ____________

Chapter 2: With what will the Lord consume "that Wicked" (antichrist)?

____

Chapter 3: In what did Paul tell them not to be weary? ____________

What does this passage mean?

How does this apply to me?

Messages preached from text:

Questions from text:

Chapter 1: Why did Paul say God put him into the ministry? ______________

Chapter 2: Was Adam deceived when he ate the fruit in the garden? ______

Chapter 3: What are three qualifications of being a pastor? ______________

Chapter 4: Why do we labor and suffer reproach? ______________

Chapter 5: Why should you rebuke those that sin before all? ______________

Chapter 6: What two things happen to those who covet money? ______________

What does this passage mean?

How does this apply to me?

Messages preached from text:

Questions from text:

Chapter 1: Who often refreshed Paul? ______________________

Chapter 2: What should we avoid because it causes strife? __________

____

Chapter 3: List three things that Timothy knew about Paul: __________

____

Chapter 4: "The time will come when they will not endure __________

______________."

What does this passage mean?

How does this apply to me?

Messages preached from text:

Questions from text:

Chapter 1: What should an elder hold fast? ______________________

Chapter 2: What verses are an exhortation to servants? ______________

Chapter 3: Who did Paul say to reject after the first and second admonition?

____

Philemon: Who did Paul say, "I have begotten in my bonds"? ____________

What does this passage mean?

How does this apply to me?

Messages preached from text:

Questions from text:

Chapter 1: By whom did God speak in times past to the fathers? __________
Chapter 2: What caused Jesus to taste death for every man? ____________

____

Chapter 3: Of whom does it say twice, "was faithful in all his house"?

____

Chapter 4: Jesus was "tempted like as we are, yet ___________ ________*."*
Chapter 5: To whom does strong meat belong? ________________________
Chapter 6: Through what two things did they inherit the promises? ________

____

What does this passage mean?

How does this apply to me?

Messages preached from text:

Questions from text:

Chapter 7: What made nothing perfect? ______________________________
Chapter 8: Moses was to make all things for the tabernacle according to the ____________________.
Chapter 9: What is appointed unto men? ______________________________
Chapter 10: What "is a fearful thing"? ______________________________

What does this passage mean?

How does this apply to me?

Messages preached from text:

Questions from text:

Chapter 11: Who was dead, but yet "speaketh"? ______________________

Chapter 12: What should you do, "lest ye be wearied and faint in your minds"?

____

Chapter 13: What are three things that you should do to them that have the rule over you? ______________________________________

What does this passage mean?

How does this apply to me?

Messages preached from text:

Questions from text:

Chapter 1: With whom is no variableness? ______________________
Chapter 2: What two Old Testament Bible characters are used to illustrate faith with works? ______________________
Chapter 3: Who is made after the similitude of God? ______________________
Chapter 4: Of whom should we not speak evil? ______________________
Chapter 5: If you are afflicted (to undergo hardship), what are you supposed to do? ______________________

What does this passage mean?

How does this apply to me?

Messages preached from text:

Questions from text:

Chapter 1: What liveth and abideth forever? ____________________
Chapter 2: Have ye tasted that the Lord is ________________*?*
Chapter 3: To accomplish the will of God, it is better to suffer for ________ *doing, than for* ____________ *doing.*
Chapter 4: What does charity cover? ____________________
Chapter 5: To whom did Peter tell the younger to submit? ____________

What does this passage mean?

How does this apply to me?

Messages preached from text:

Questions from text:

Chapter 1: What would be multiplied through the knowledge of God? ______

______

Chapter 2: Who loved the wages of unrighteousness? ______

Chapter 3: Who did Peter call "our beloved brother"? ______

What does this passage mean?

How does this apply to me?

Messages preached from text:

Questions from text:

Chapter 1: Who do we deceive if we say we have no sin? ______________

Chapter 2: What "abideth forever"? ______________

Chapter 3: "Sin is the ______________ ______ __________ __________."

Chapter 4: Why do we love Him? ______________

Chapter 5: What did He say ye may know? ______________

What does this passage mean?

How does this apply to me?

Messages preached from text:

Questions from text:

II John: What kind of reward should we seek to receive? ______________

III John: What should we not follow? ______________

Jude: Who is described as sensual, not having the spirit? ______________

____

What does this passage mean?

How does this apply to me?

Messages preached from text:

Questions from text:

Chapter 1: What keys does the Son of Man hold? ____________________

Chapter 2: What church was located where Satan's seat was? ____________________

Chapter 3: In what verses do you find, "hear what the Spirit saith"? ______

Chapter 4: The four beasts give __________________ *and* ______________ *and* ____________________ *to Him that sat on the throne.*

What does this passage mean?

How does this apply to me?

Messages preached from text:

Questions from text:

Chapter 5: The Lamb (Jesus) hast made us unto our God ________________ and __________________________.

Chapter 6: What was compared to a fig tree casting her untimely figs?

____

Chapter 7: "God shall wipe away _________ ___________ from their eyes."

Chapter 8: During what trumpet did a third part of the sea turn to blood?

____

Chapter 9: In what river were four angels bound? ________________________

What does this passage mean?

How does this apply to me?

Messages preached from text:

Questions from text:

Chapter 10: Upon what was the feet of the mighty angel set? ____________

____

Chapter 11: Who shall kill the two witnesses? ____________

Chapter 12: Who is the accuser of the brethren? ____________

Chapter 13: "All the ____________ wondered after the beast."

Chapter 14: "____________ are the dead which die in the Lord."

What does this passage mean?

How does this apply to me?

Messages preached from text:

Questions from text:

Chapter 15: What two words describe God's works? ____________________

____

Chapter 16: In what three verses is the word "blasphemed" used? ________

Chapter 17: What three things are mentioned about these that are with the Lamb? ____

Chapter 18: What would not be "found any more" in Babylon? __________

____

What does this passage mean?

How does this apply to me?

Messages preached from text:

Questions from text:

Chapter 19: "Blessed are they which are called unto" what? ______________

____

Chapter 20: Who will Satan gather to battle that "numbers as the sand of the sea"? ______________

Chapter 21: What will light the New Jerusalem? ______________

____

Chapter 22: What tree in Heaven is mentioned? ______________

What does this passage mean?

How does this apply to me?

Messages preached from text: